D1216319

YOU
CAN'T
GET
THERE
FROM
HERE

Other books by Jason from Fantagraphics

HEY, WAIT...

THE IRON WAGON
(based upon the novel by Stein Riverton)

SSHHHH!

TELL ME SOMETHING

FANTAGRAPHICS BOOKS
7563 Lake City Way NE
Seattle WA 98115

Designed by Jason
Edited and Translated by Kim Thompson
Production by Carrie Whitney and Paul Baresh
Published by Gary Groth and Kim Thompson

Special thanks to Eivor Vindenes of Bladkompaniet.

Originally published in Norway under the title *Du Går Feil Vei.*

To receive a free catalog of comics, call 1-800-657-1100 or write us at
Fantagraphics Books, 7563 Lake City Way NE, Seattle, WA 98115.

Visit the website for Jippi, who originally publishes Jason's work,
at www.jippicomics.com
Visit the website for The Beguiling, where Jason's original artwork
can be purchased: www.beguiling.com
Visit the Fantagraphics website, just because: www.fantagraphics.com

First printing: May 2004

ISBN: 1-56097-598-9

Printed in Korea

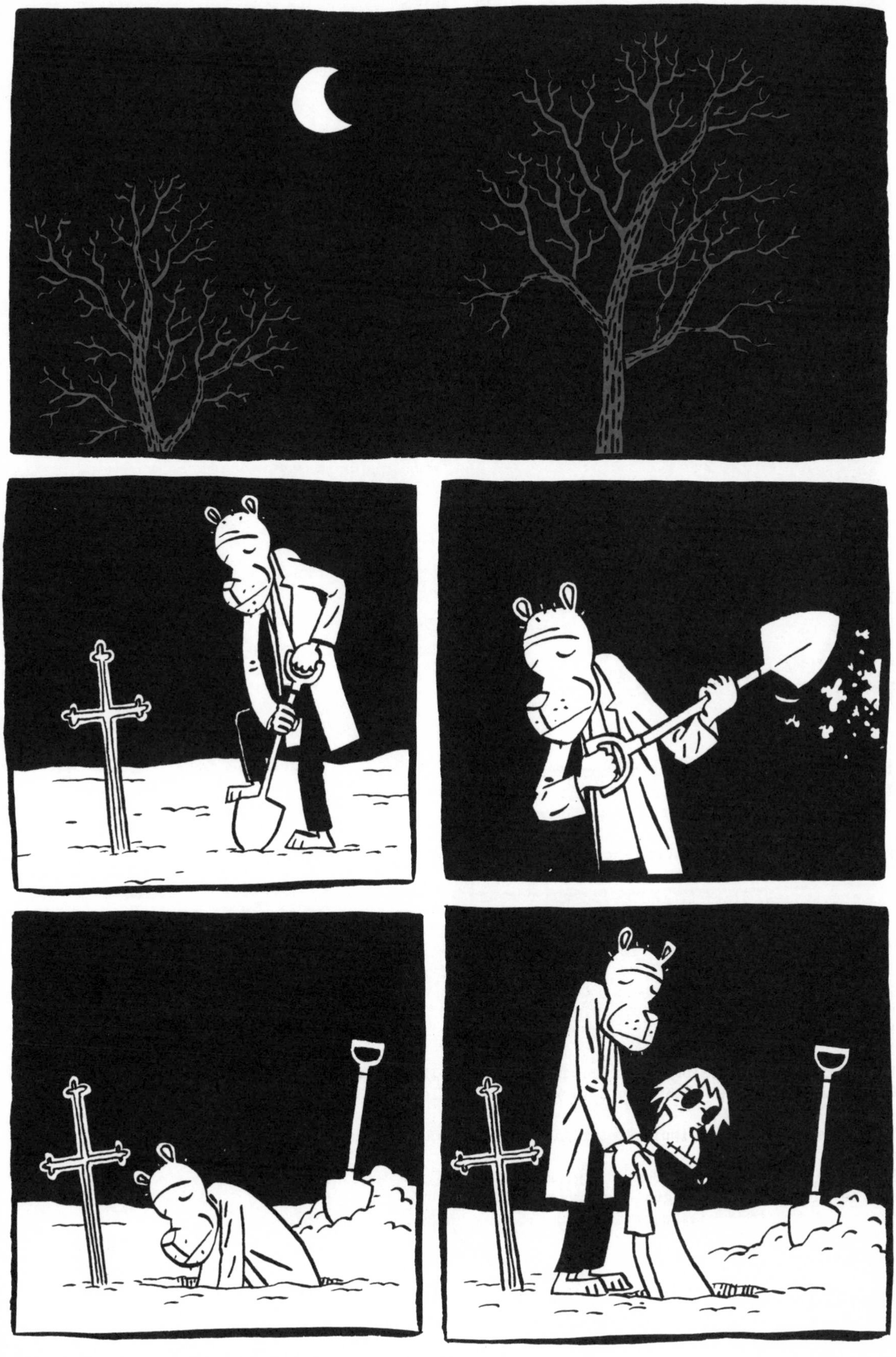

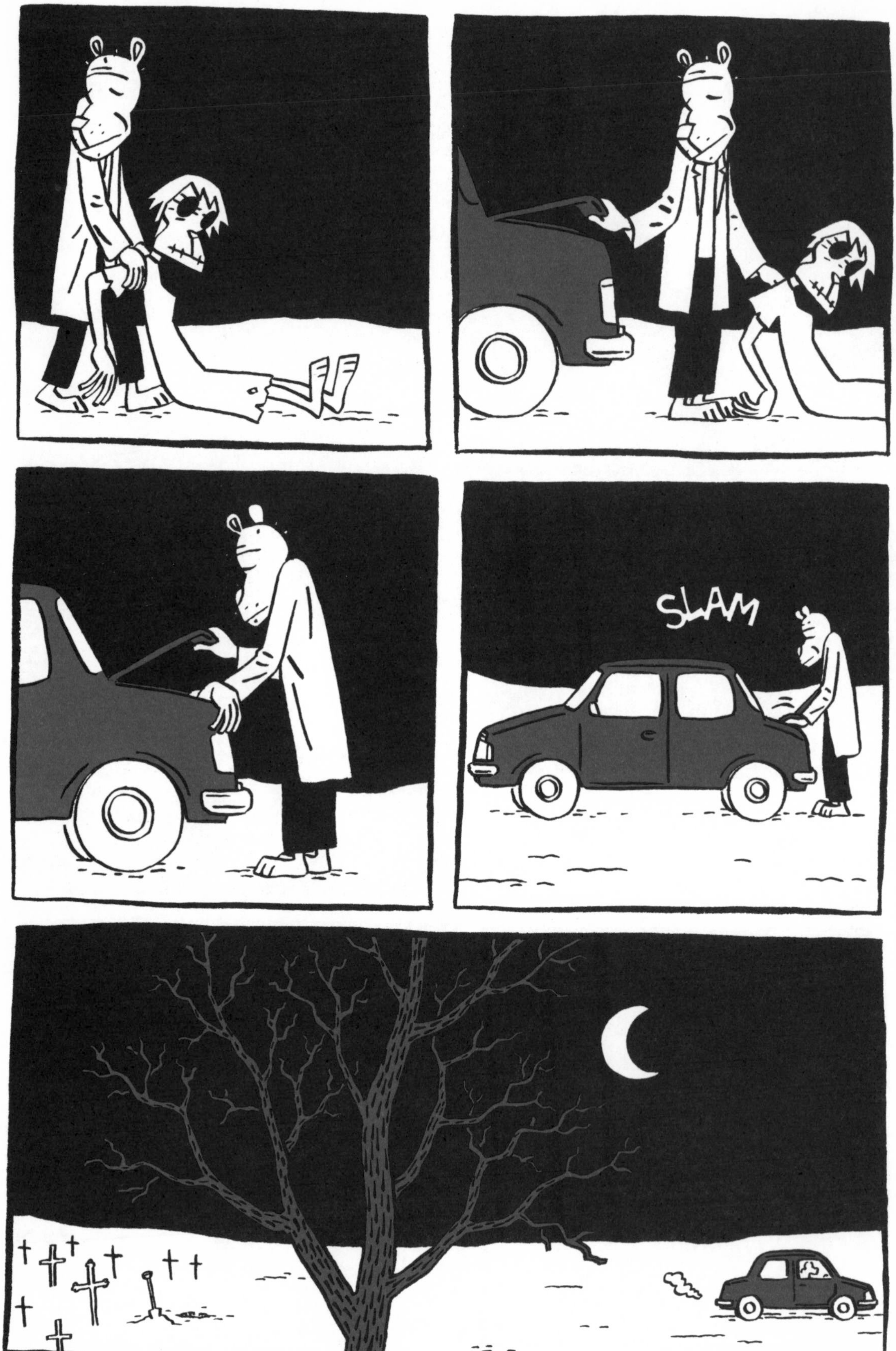
SLAM

YOU CAN'T GET THERE FROM HERE

BY JASON

FANTAGRAPHICS BOOKS

ONE

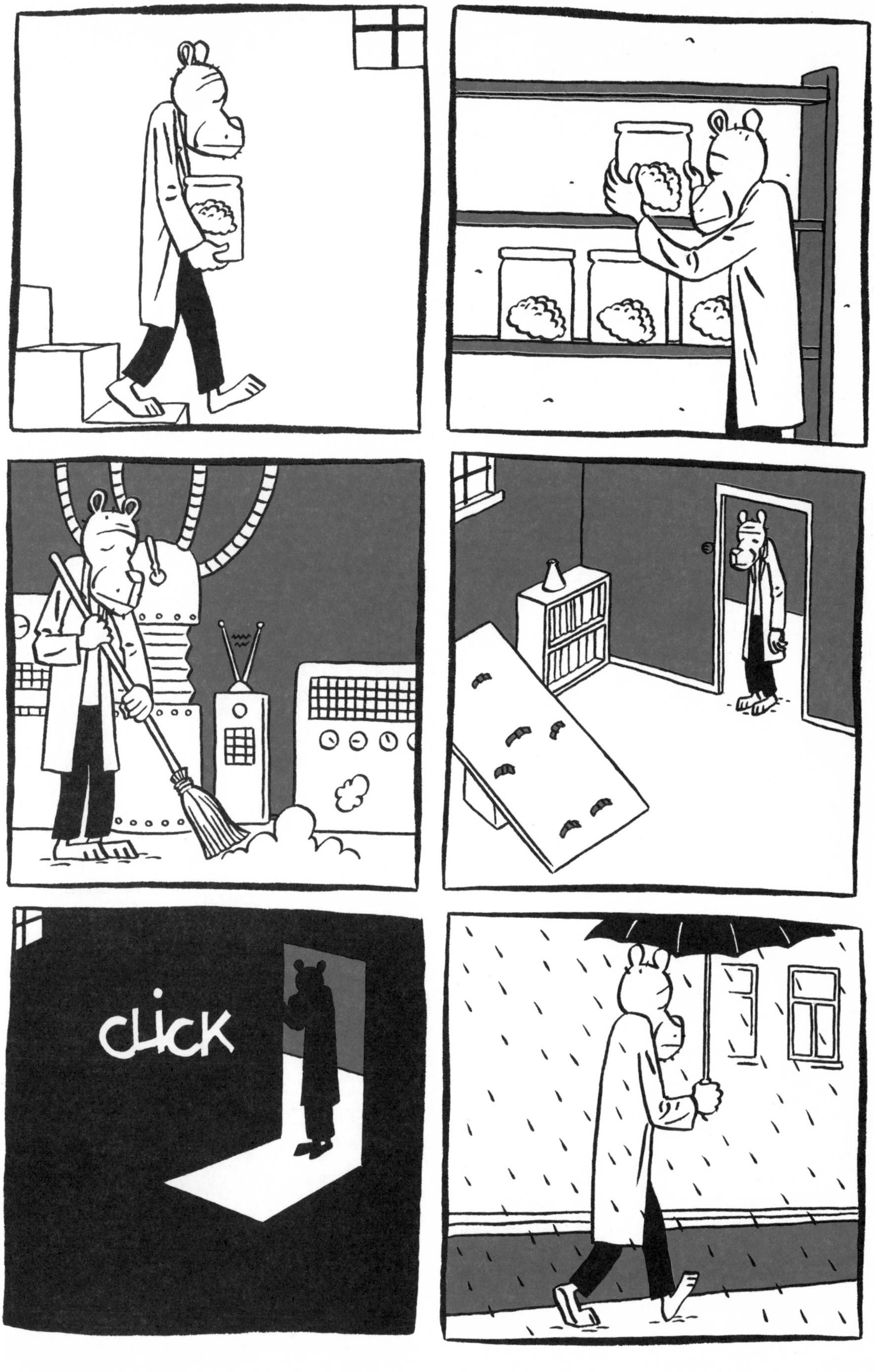
CLICK

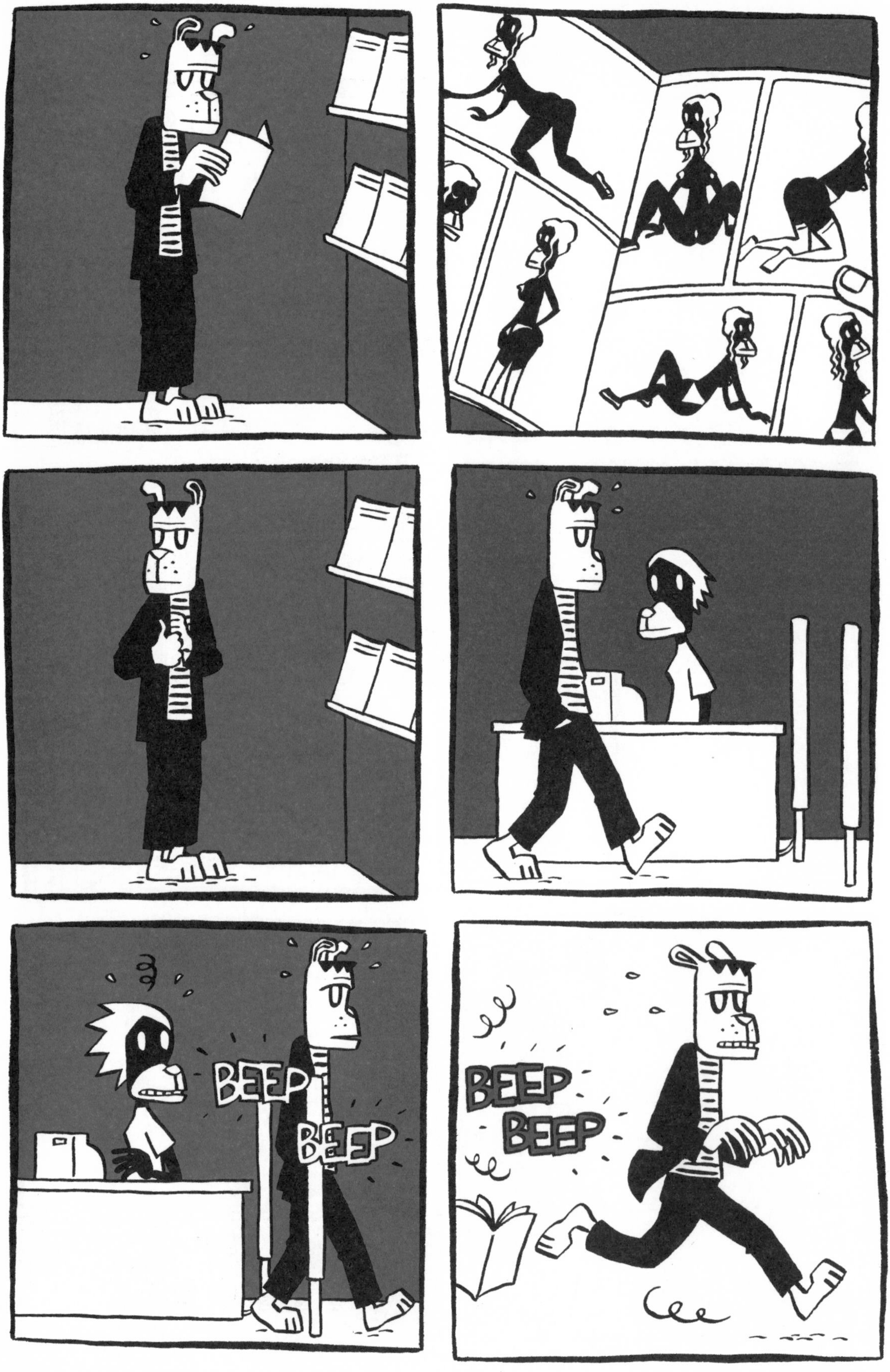
BEEP
BEEP
BEEP
BEEP

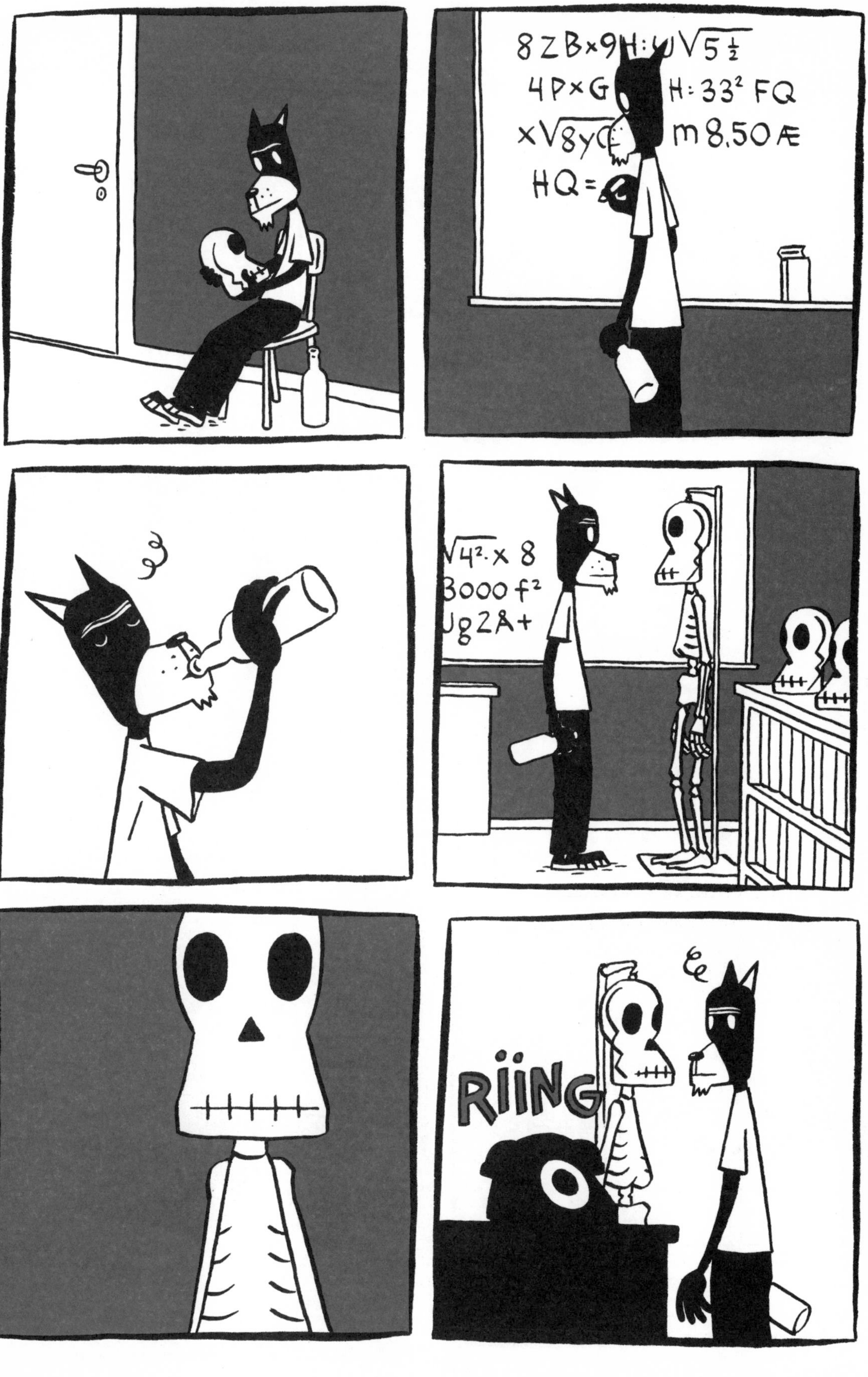
8ZB×9H:UV5½
4P×G H:33² FQ
×V8yC m8,50Æ
HQ=
V4².×8
3000 f²
Ug2Å+
RÏING

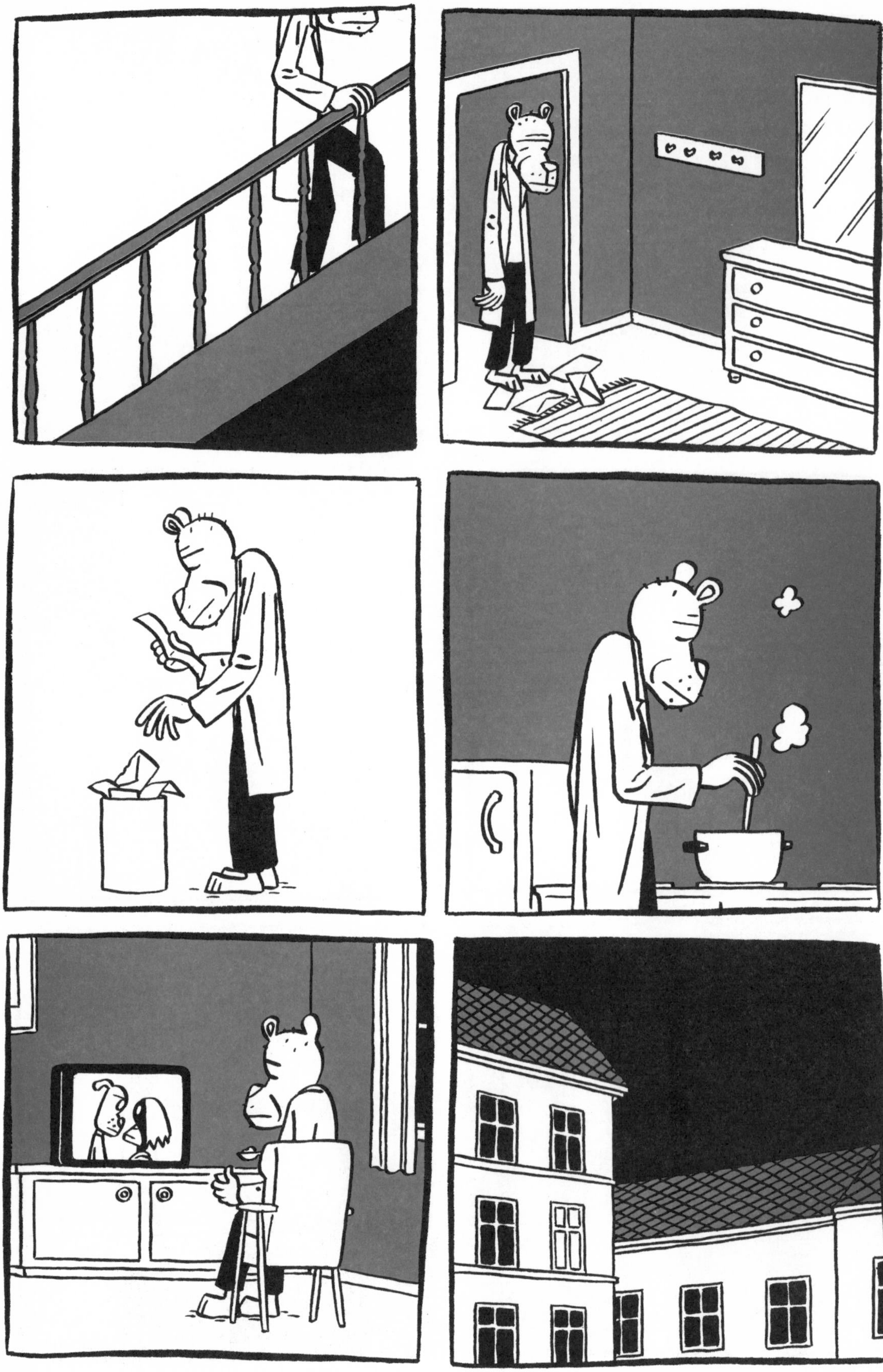

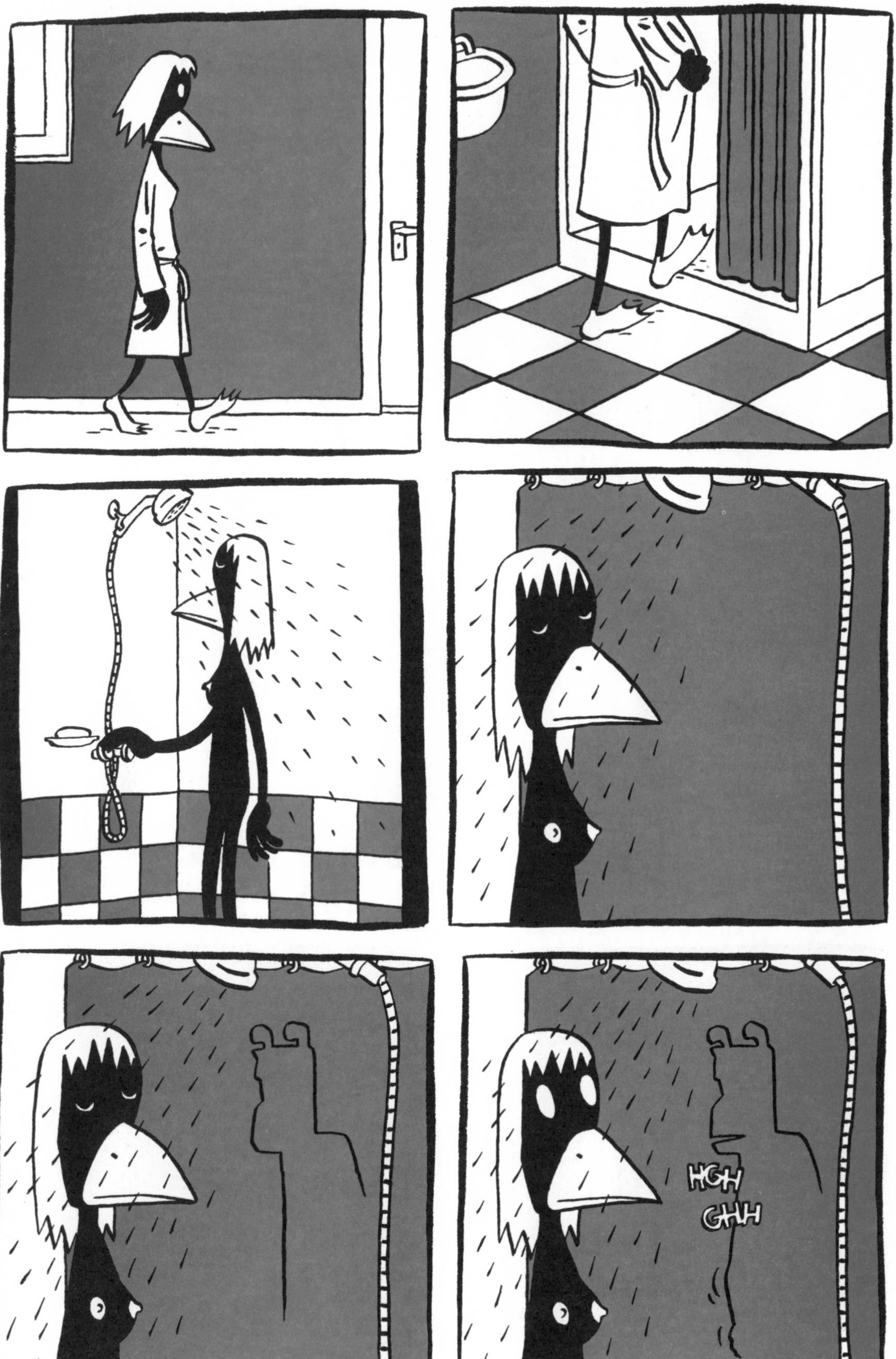
HGH
GHH

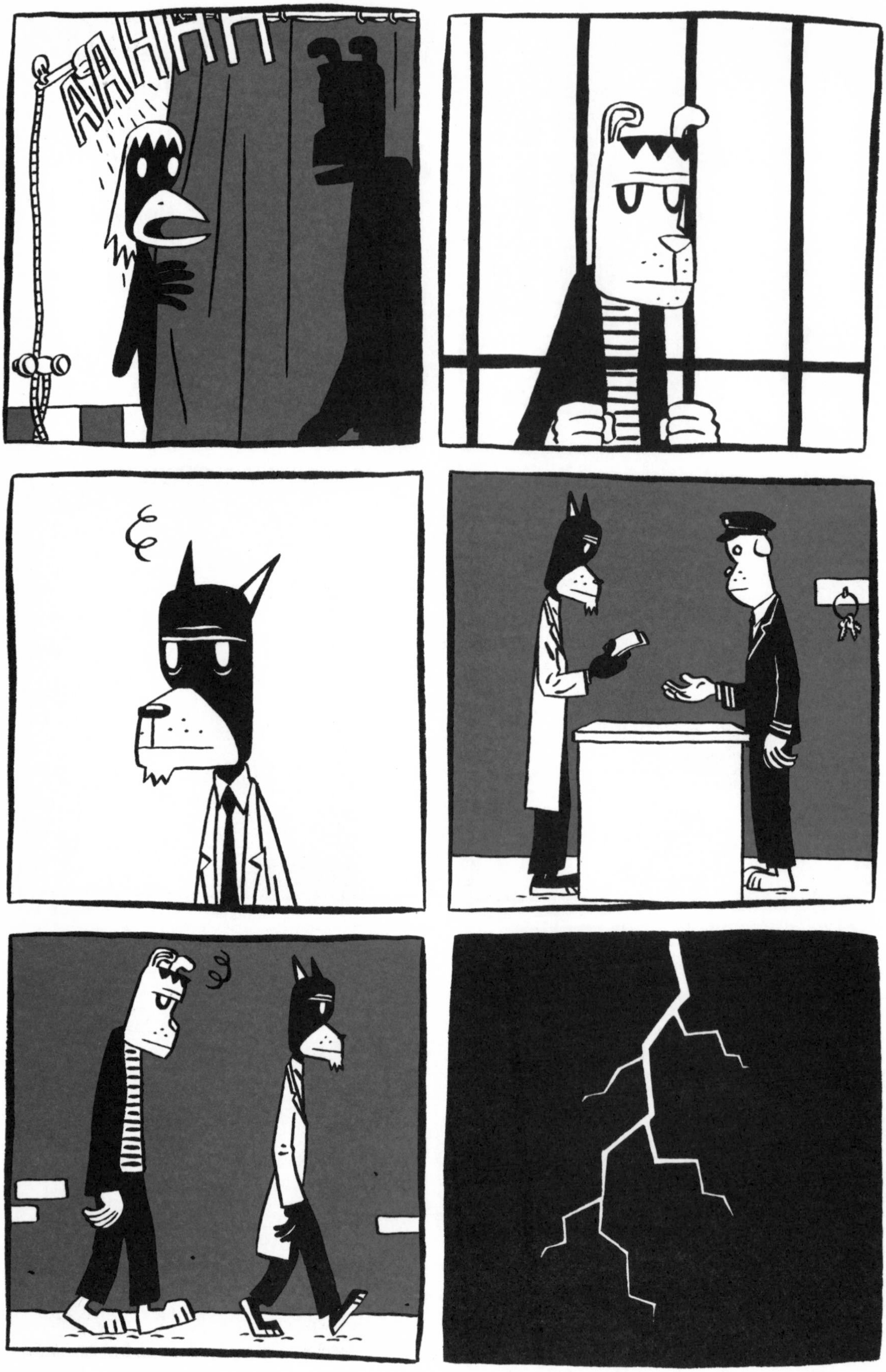
AAHHHH

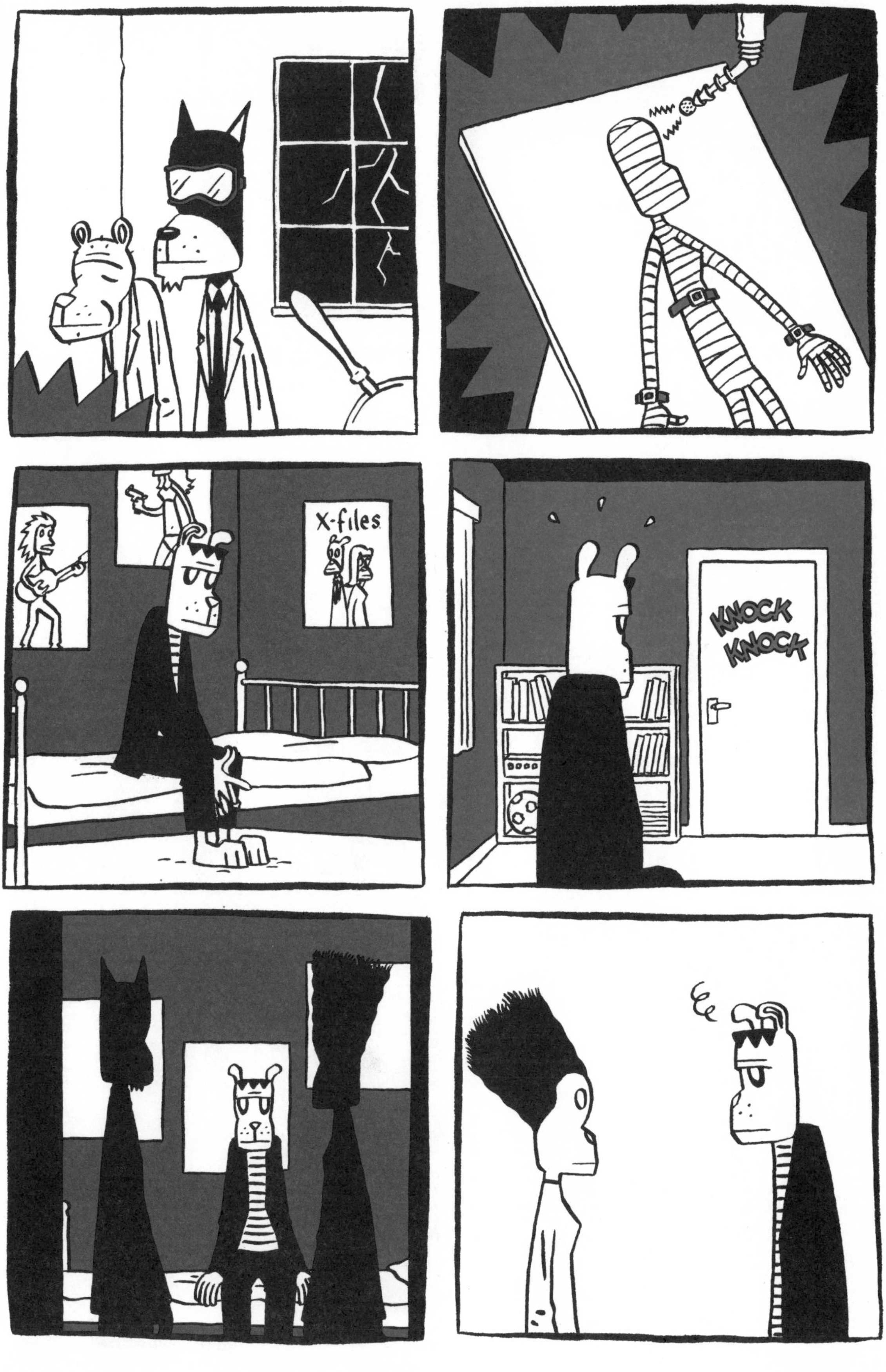
X-files
KNOCK
KNOCK

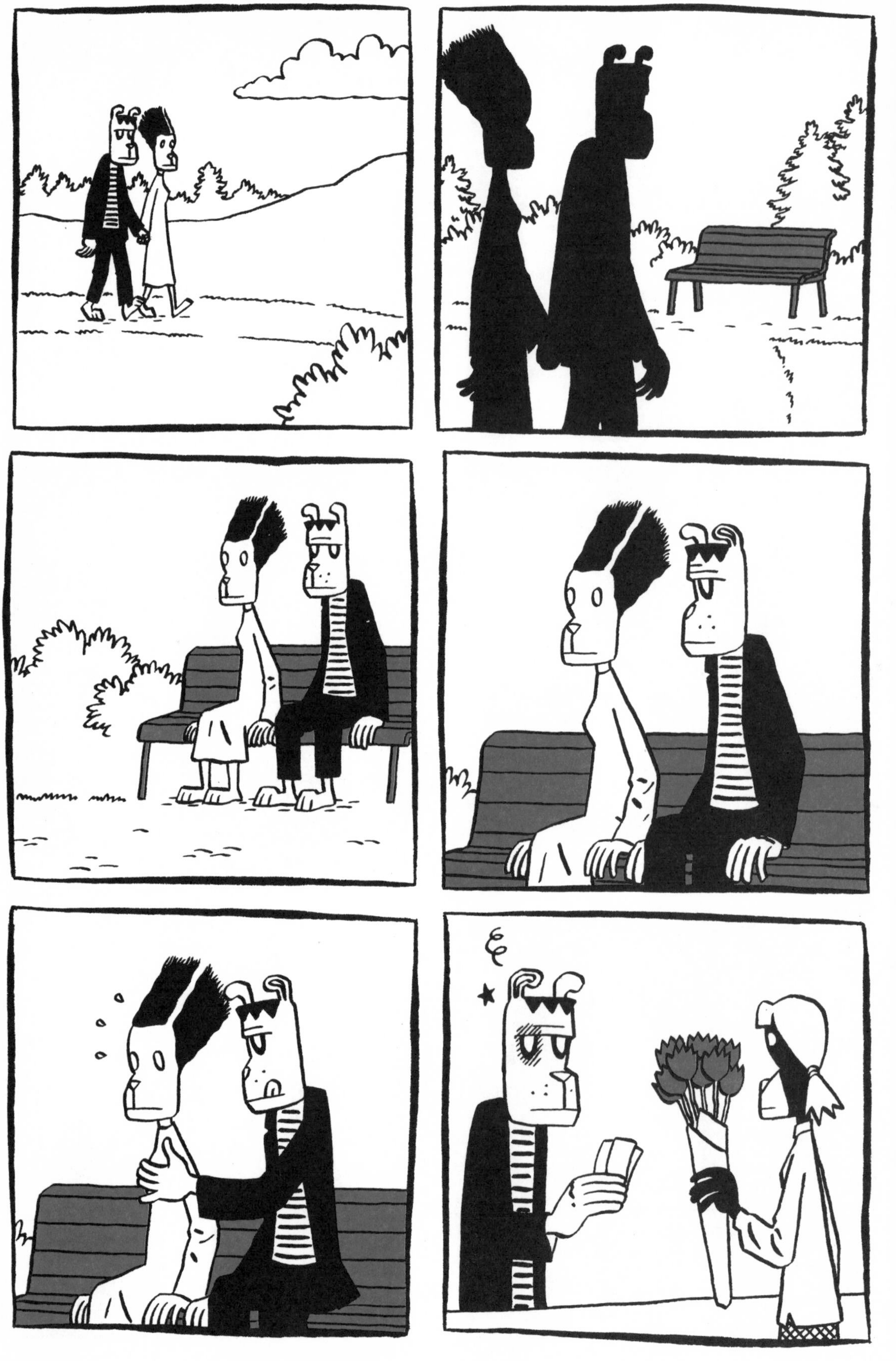

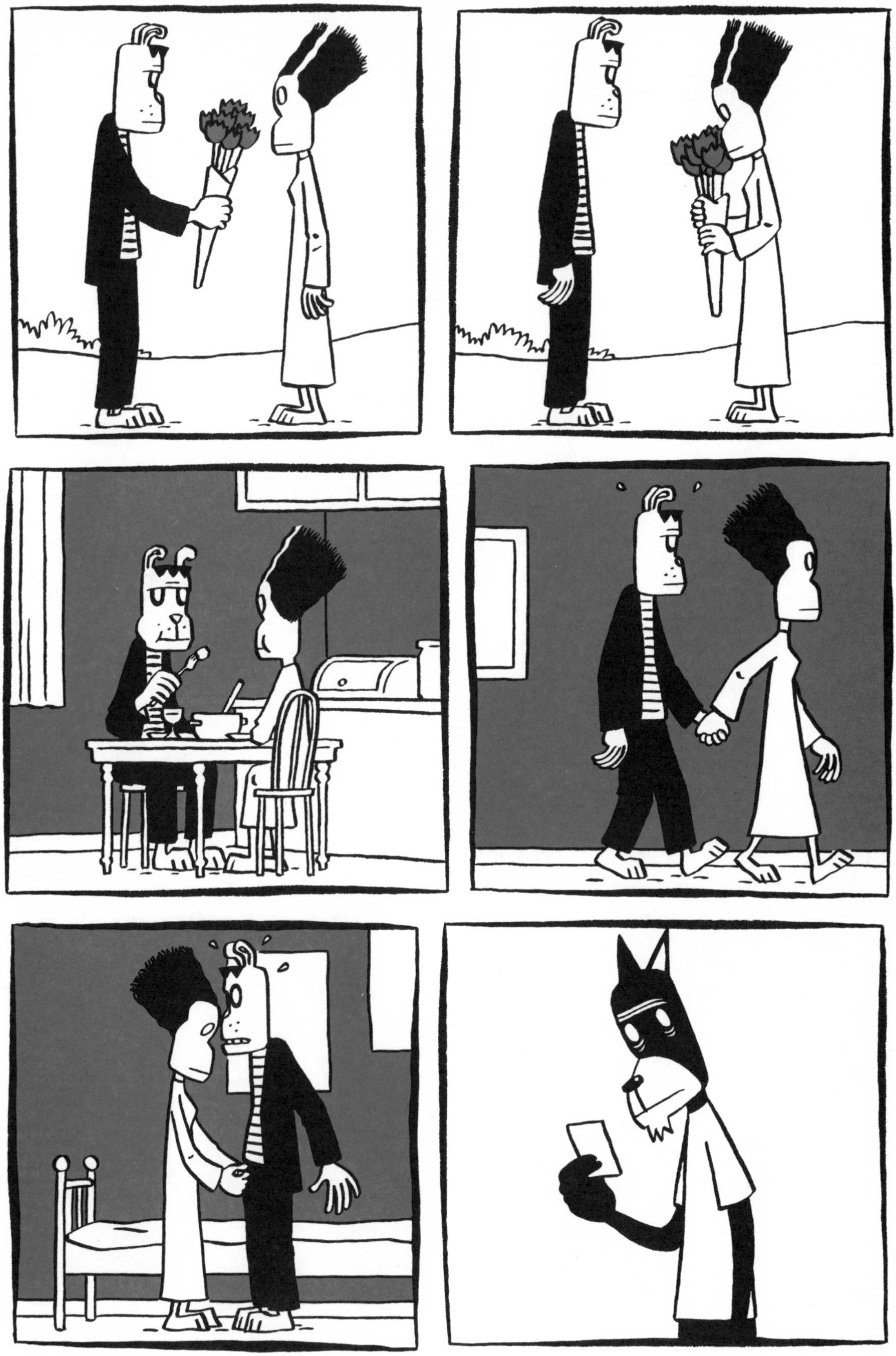

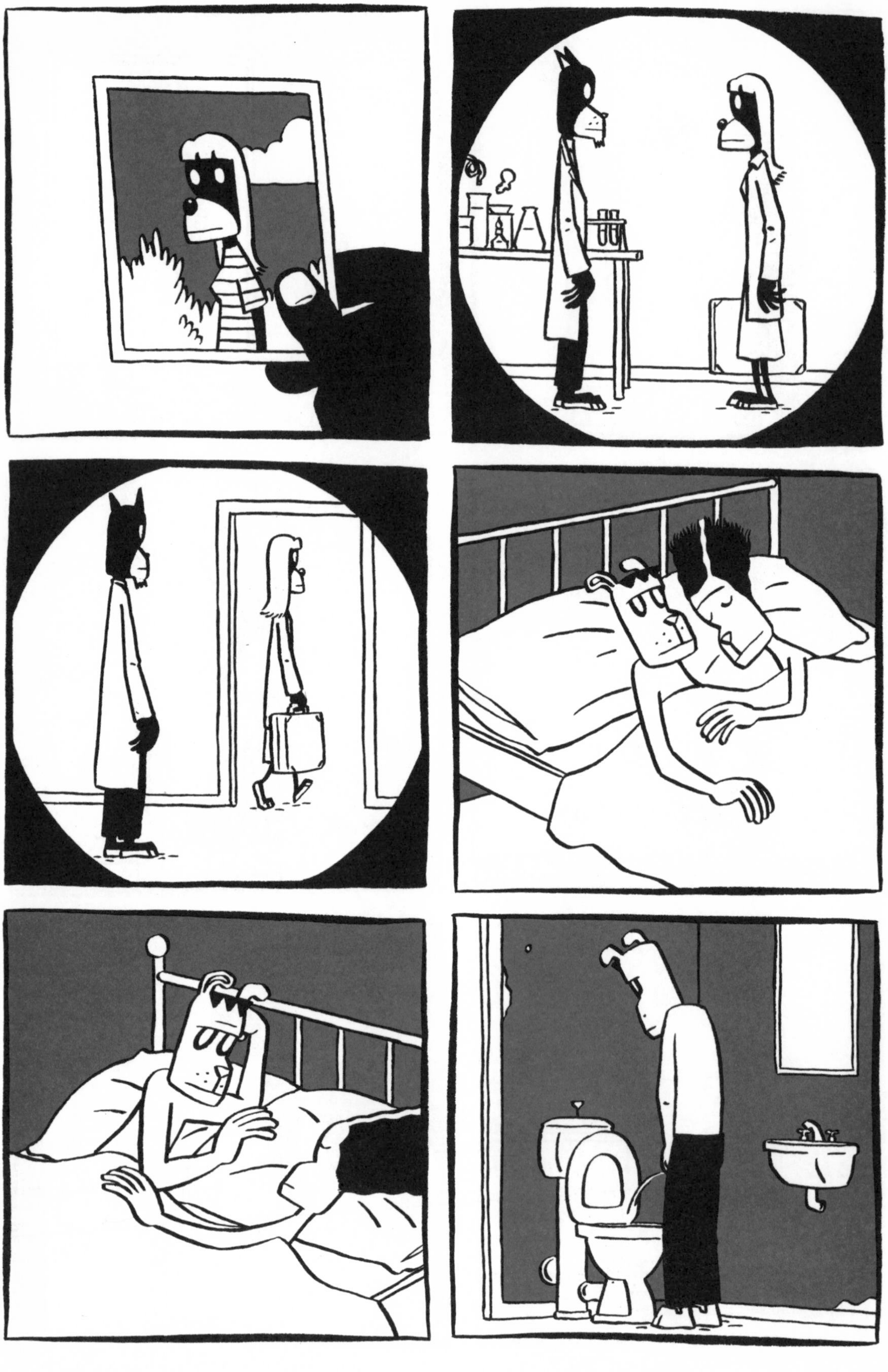

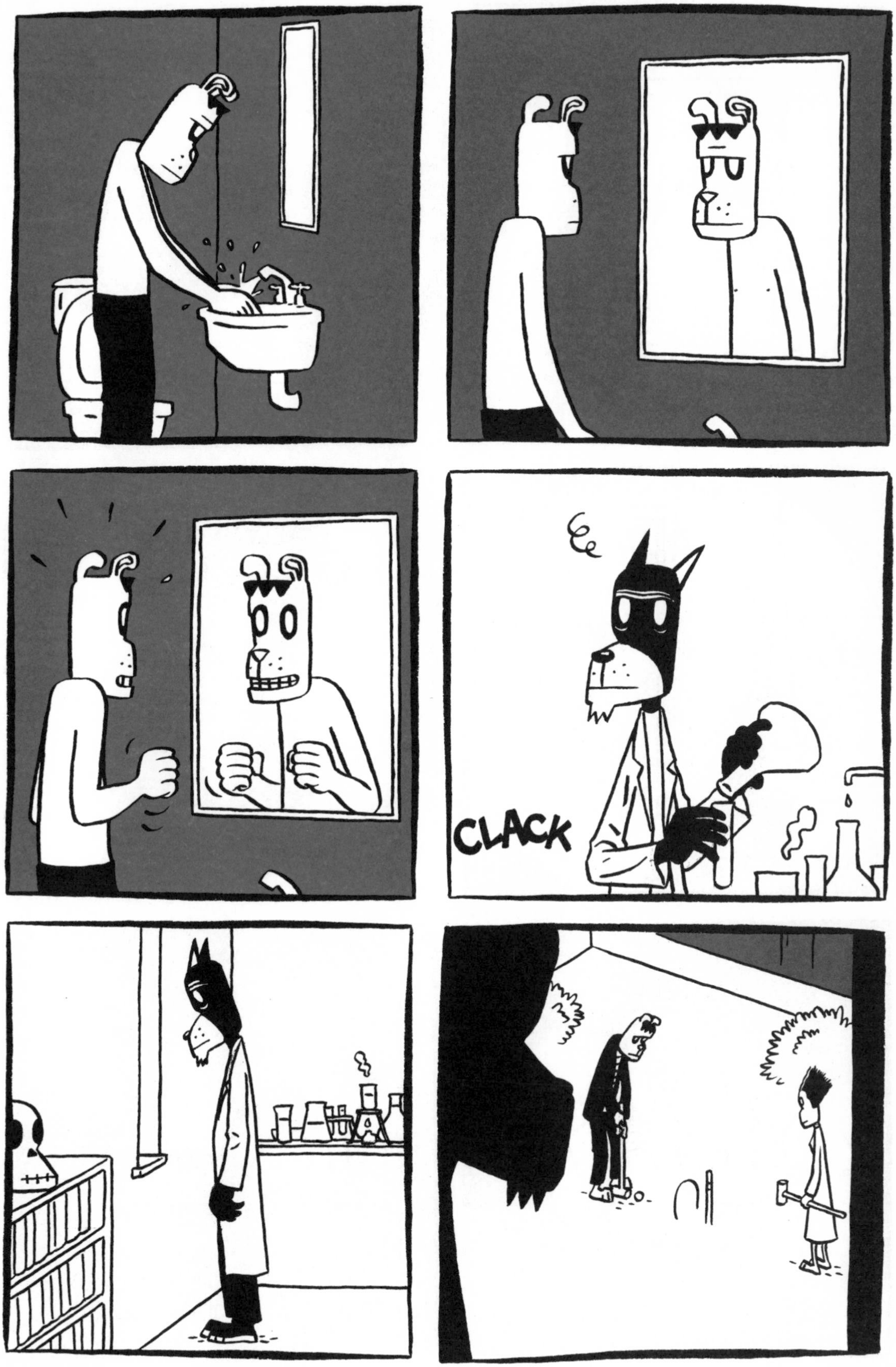
CLACK

CLACK

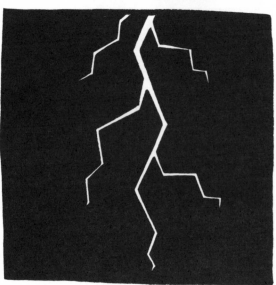

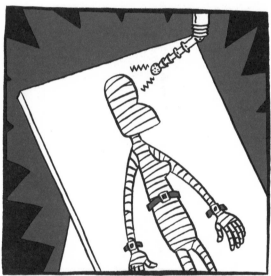

KNOCK KNOCK

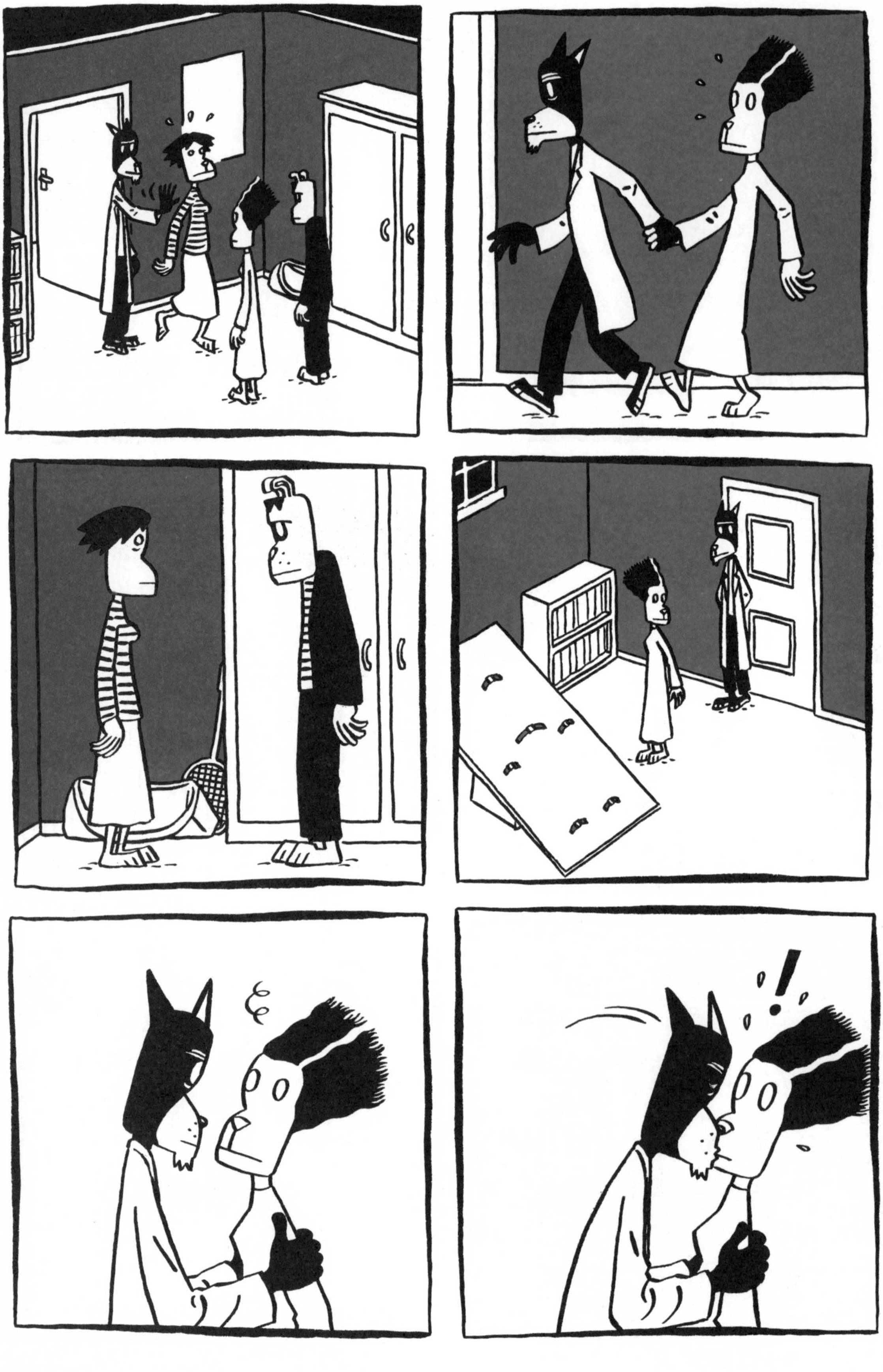
!

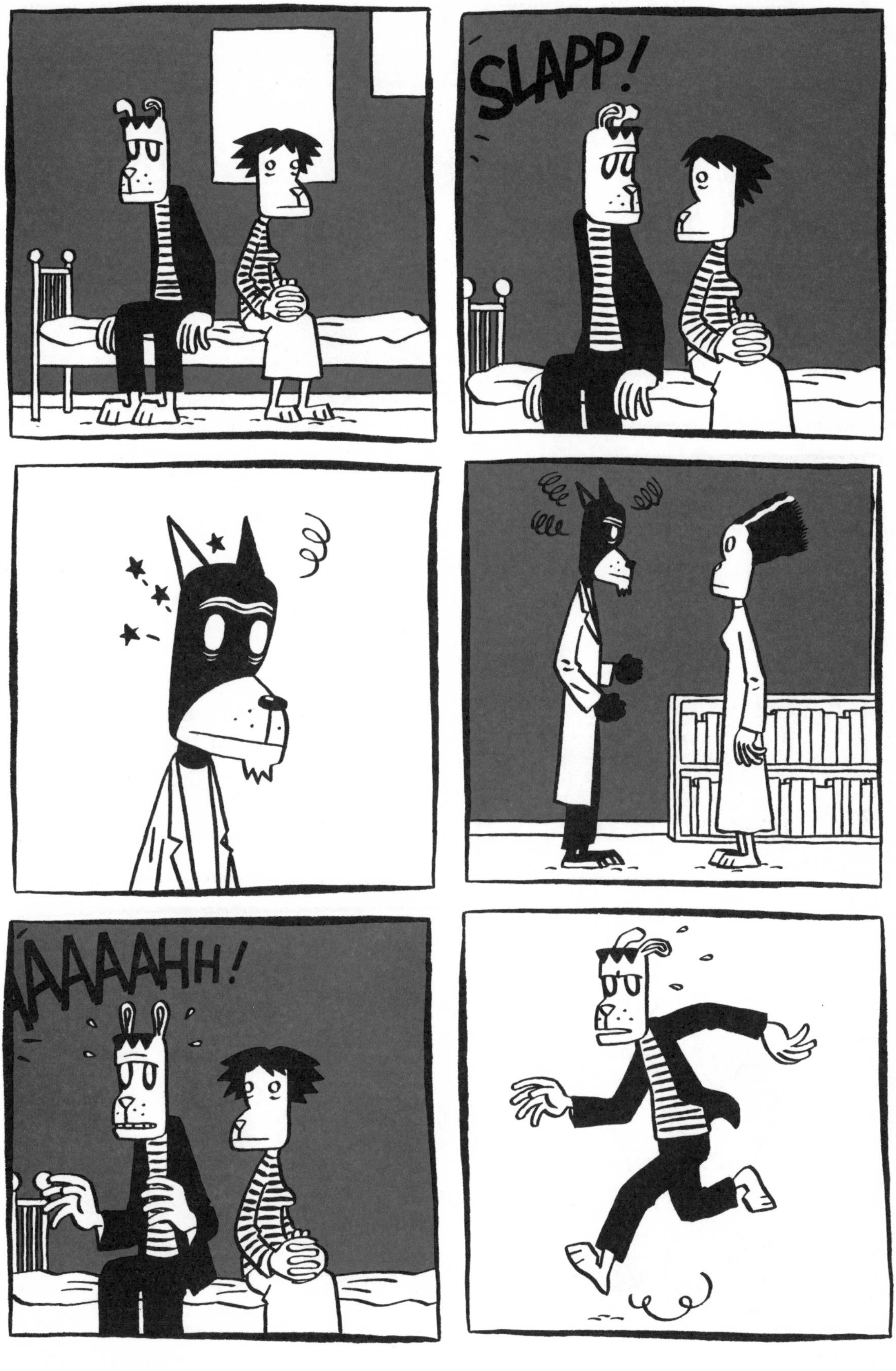
SLAPP!
AAAAAHH!

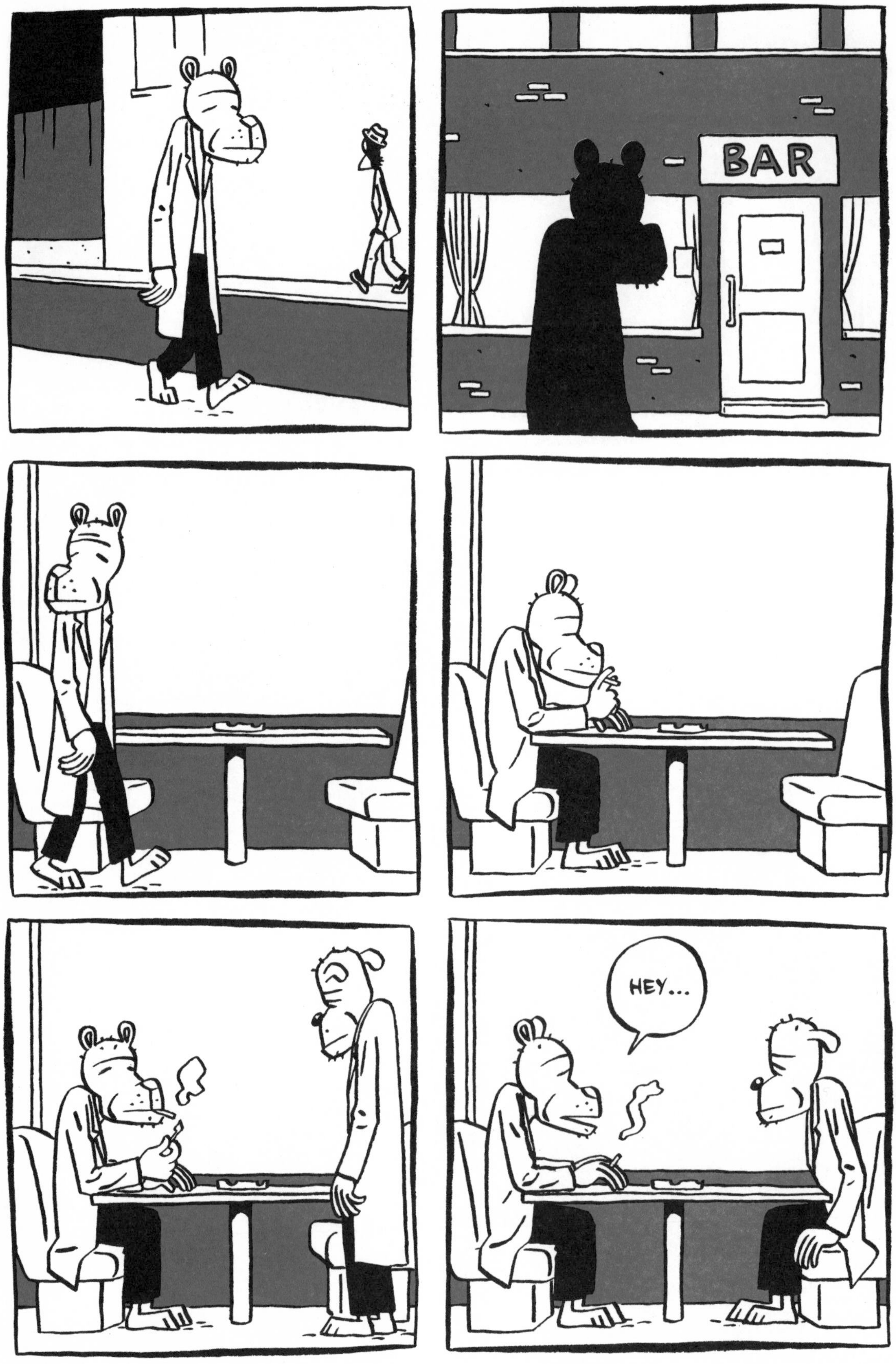
BAR
HEY...

TWO

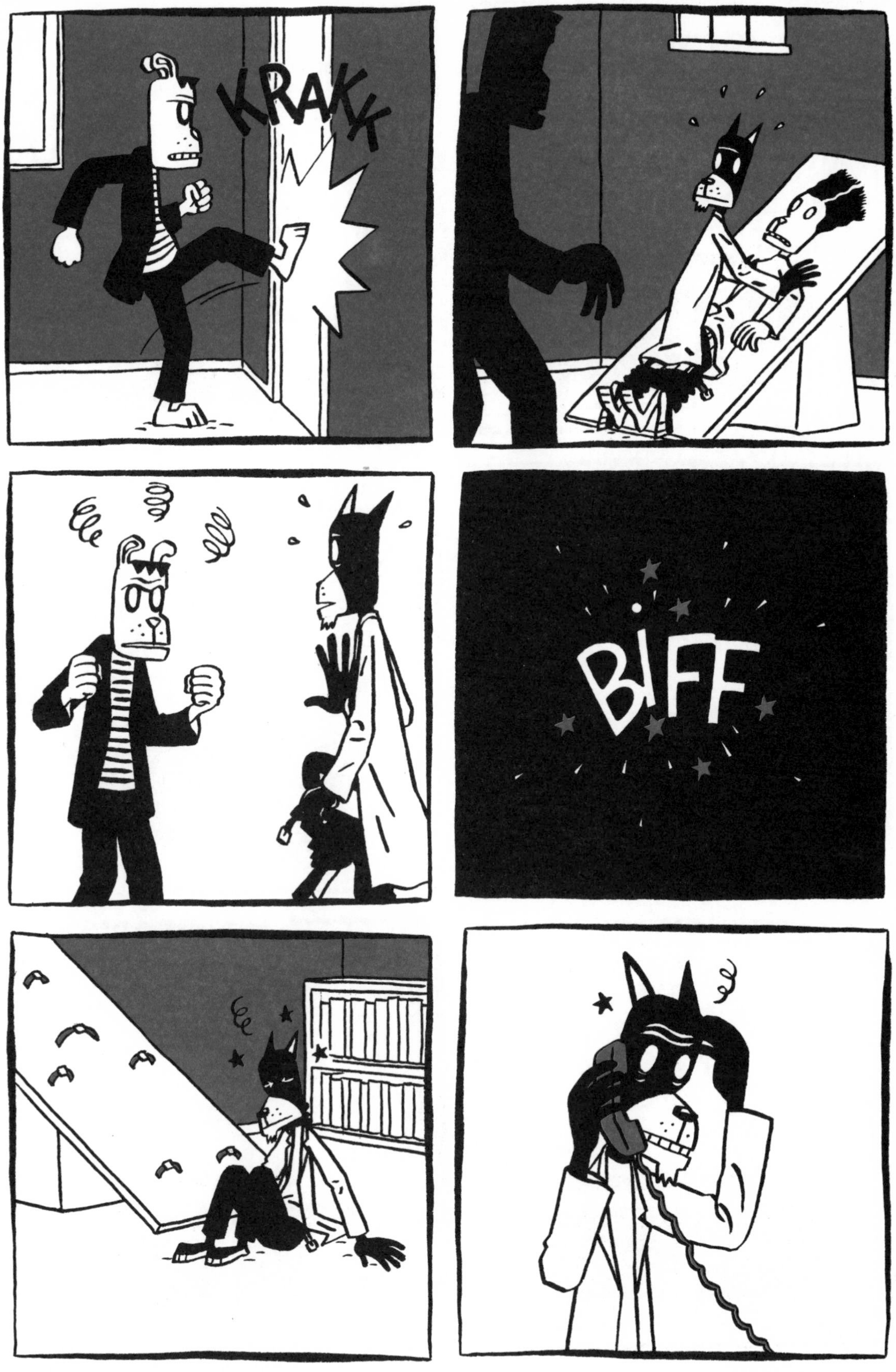
KRAKK
BIFF

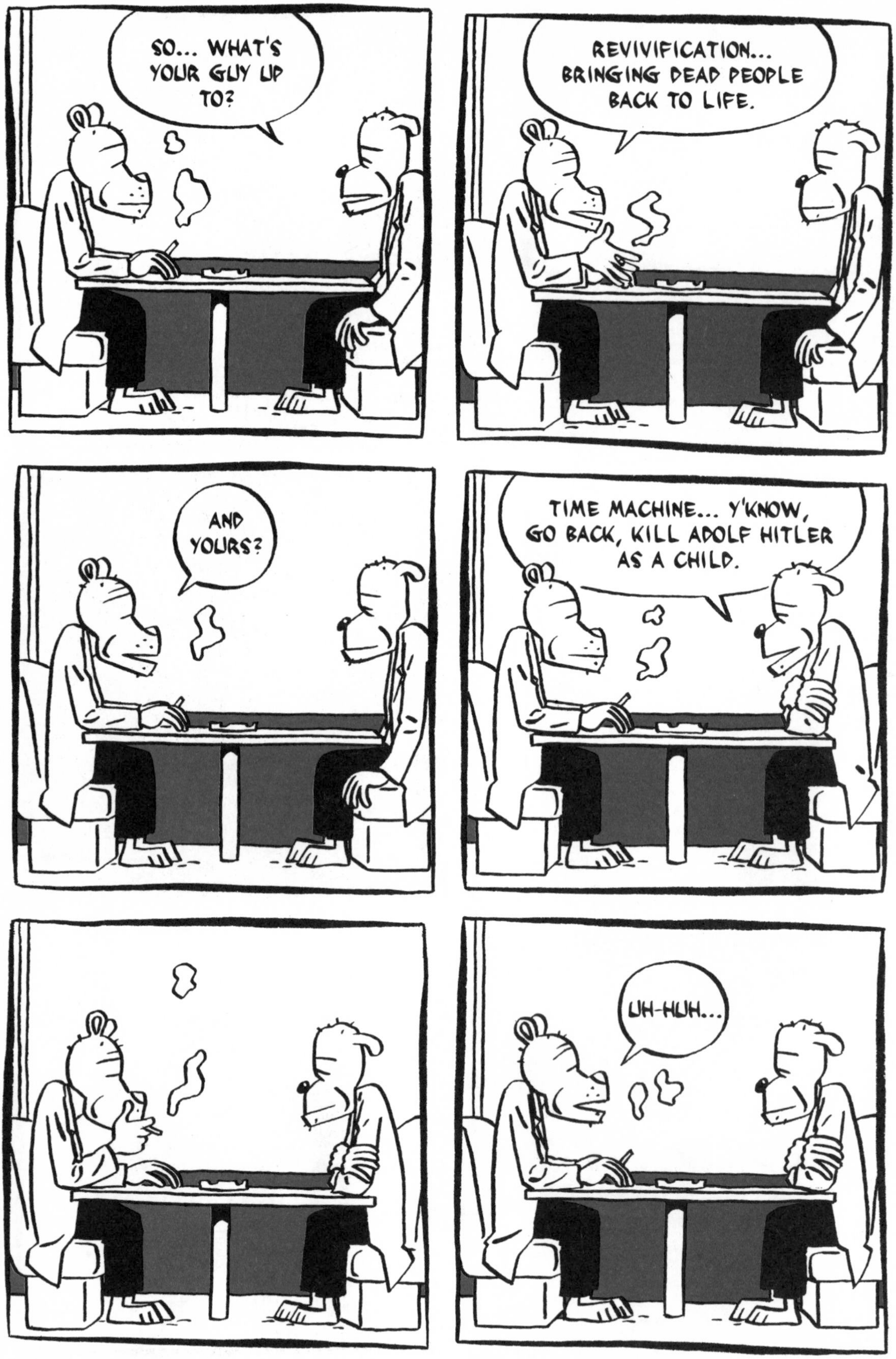
SO... WHAT'S YOUR GUY UP TO?
REVIVIFICATION... BRINGING DEAD PEOPLE BACK TO LIFE.
AND YOURS?
TIME MACHINE... Y'KNOW, GO BACK, KILL ADOLF HITLER AS A CHILD.
UH-HUH...

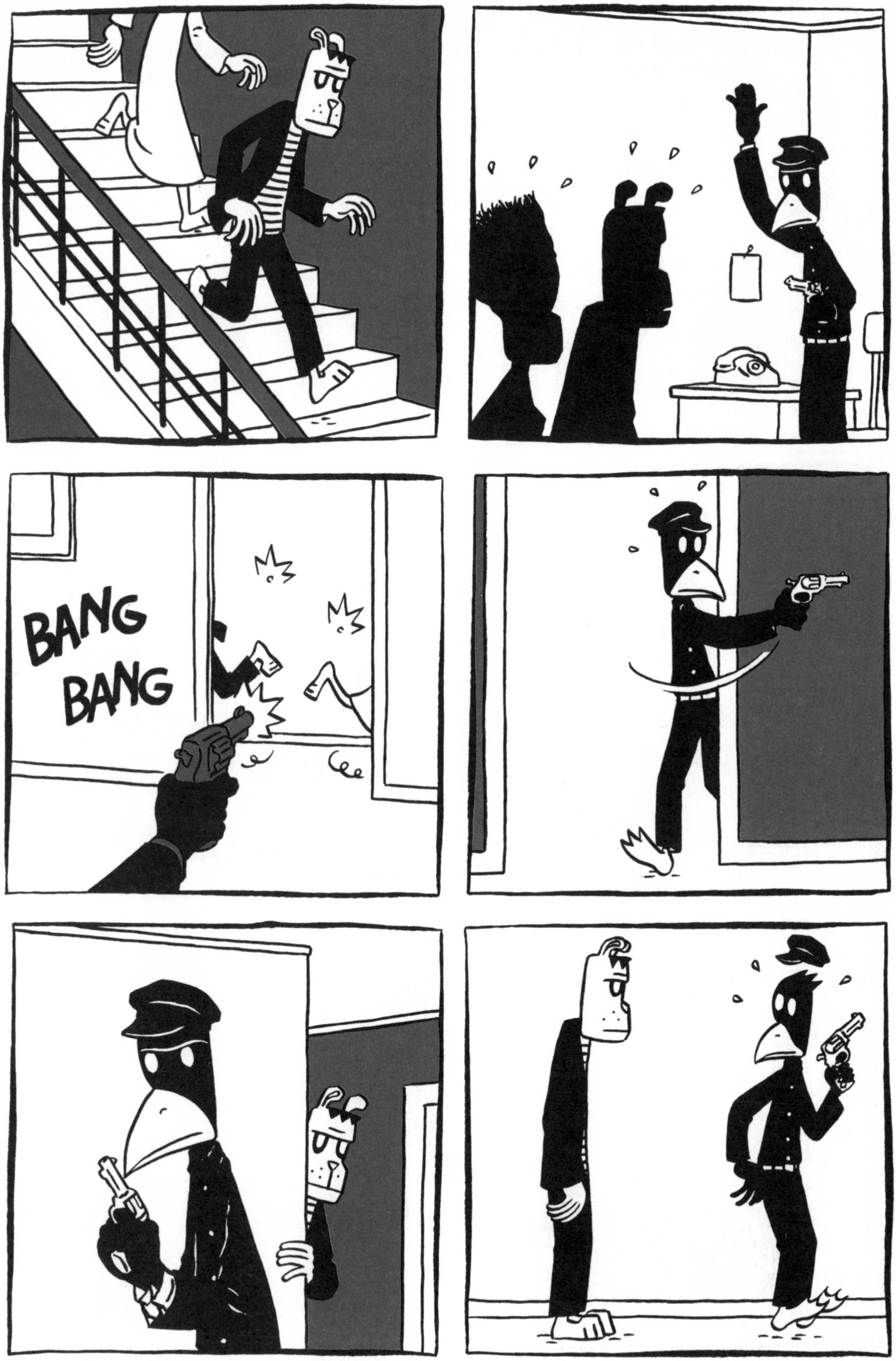
BANG
BANG

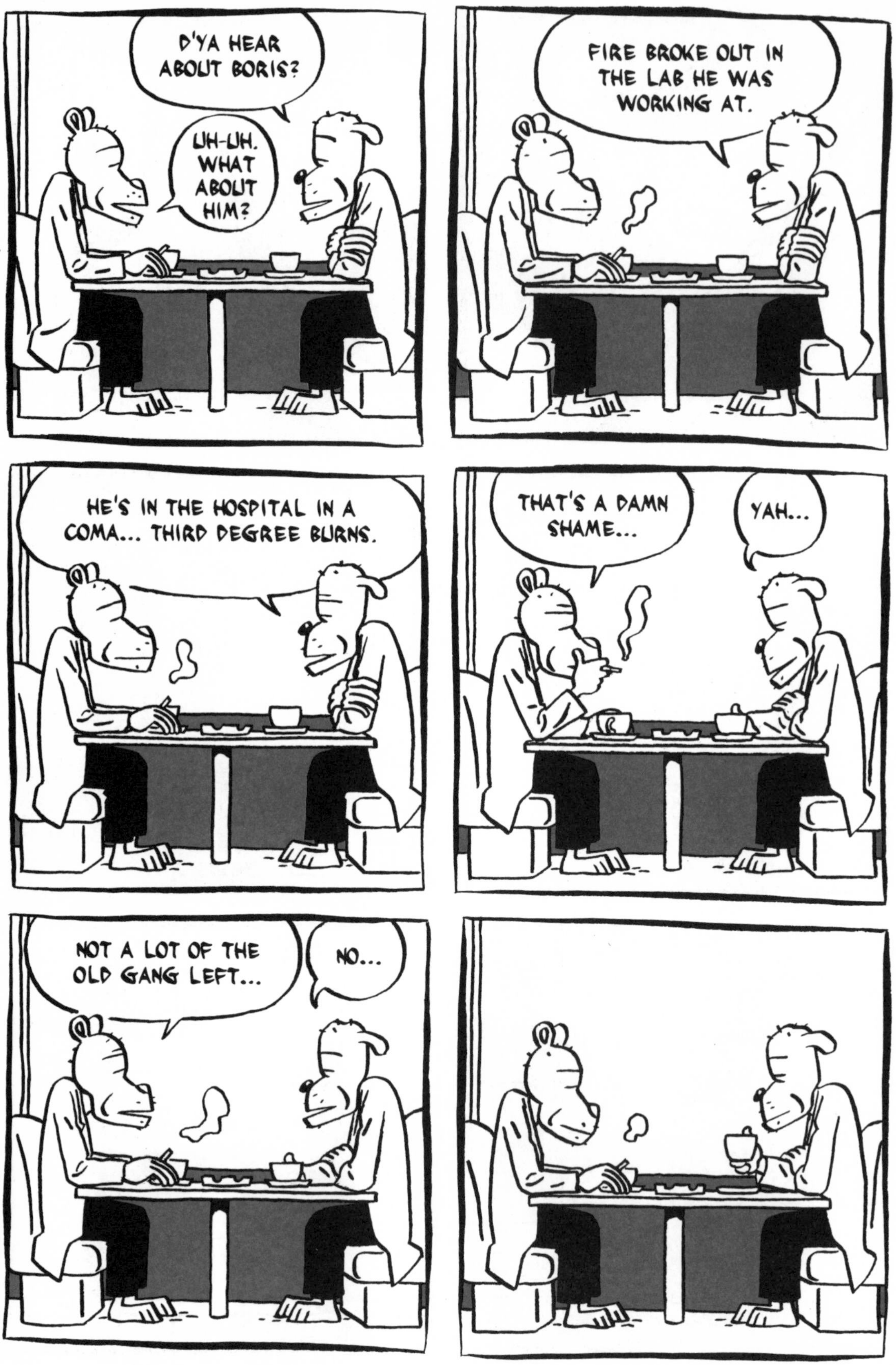
D'YA HEAR ABOUT BORIS?
UH-UH. WHAT ABOUT HIM?
FIRE BROKE OUT IN THE LAB HE WAS WORKING AT.
HE'S IN THE HOSPITAL IN A COMA... THIRD DEGREE BURNS.
THAT'S A DAMN SHAME...
YAH...
NOT A LOT OF THE OLD GANG LEFT...
NO...

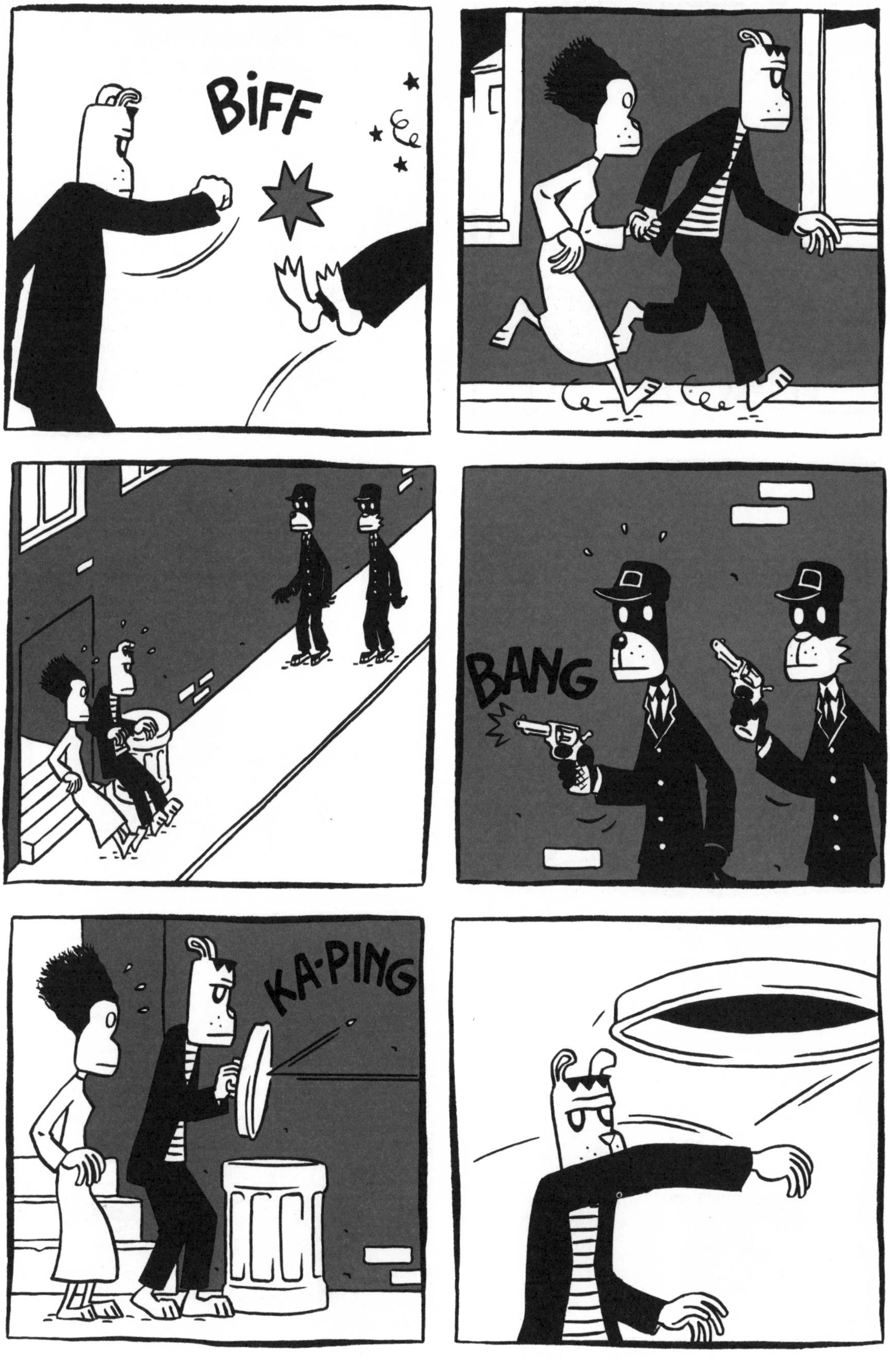
BiFF
BANG
KA-PING

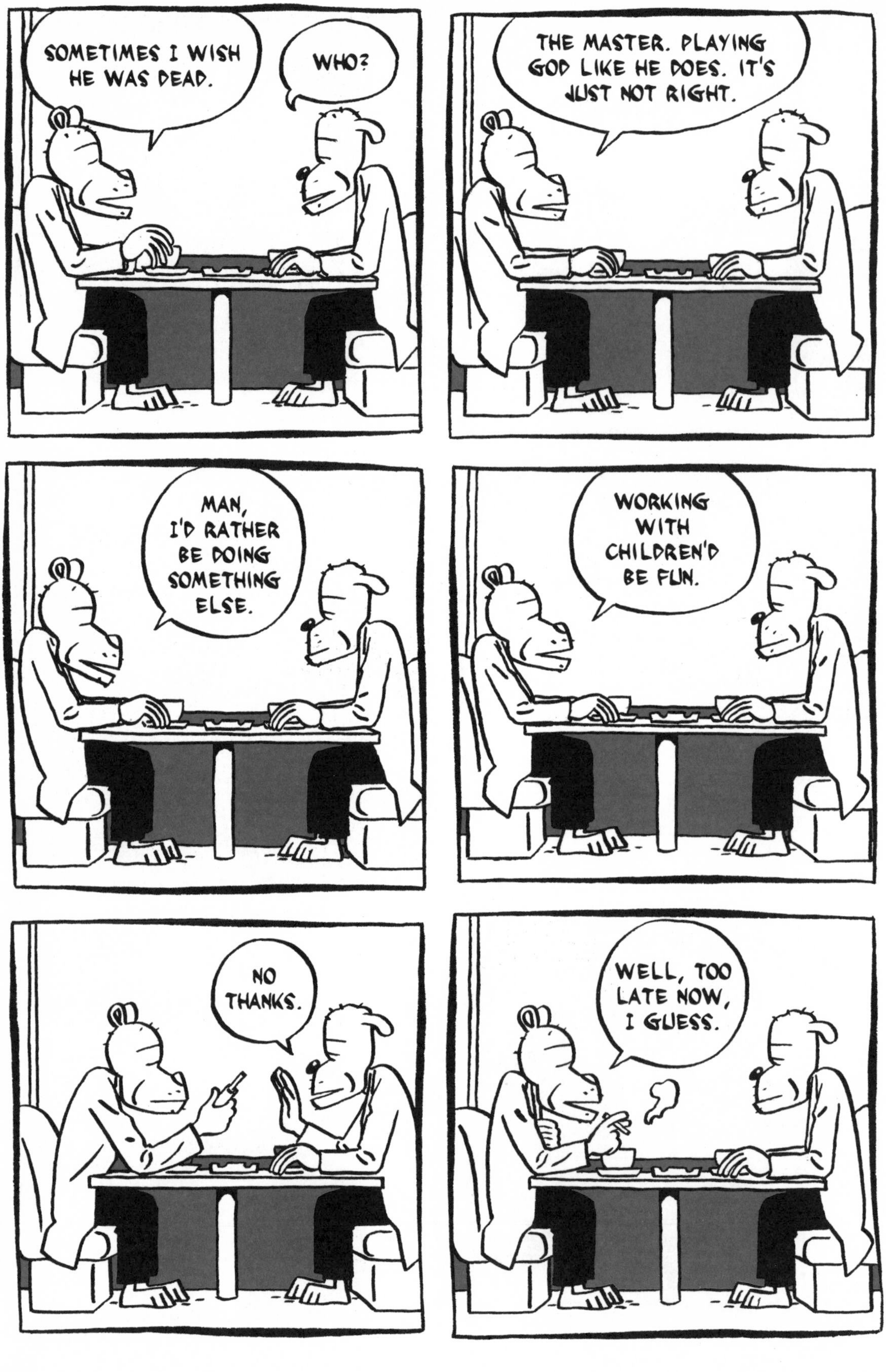
SOMETIMES I WISH HE WAS DEAD.
WHO?
THE MASTER. PLAYING GOD LIKE HE DOES. IT'S JUST NOT RIGHT.
MAN, I'D RATHER BE DOING SOMETHING ELSE.
WORKING WITH CHILDREN'D BE FUN.
NO THANKS.
WELL, TOO LATE NOW, I GUESS.

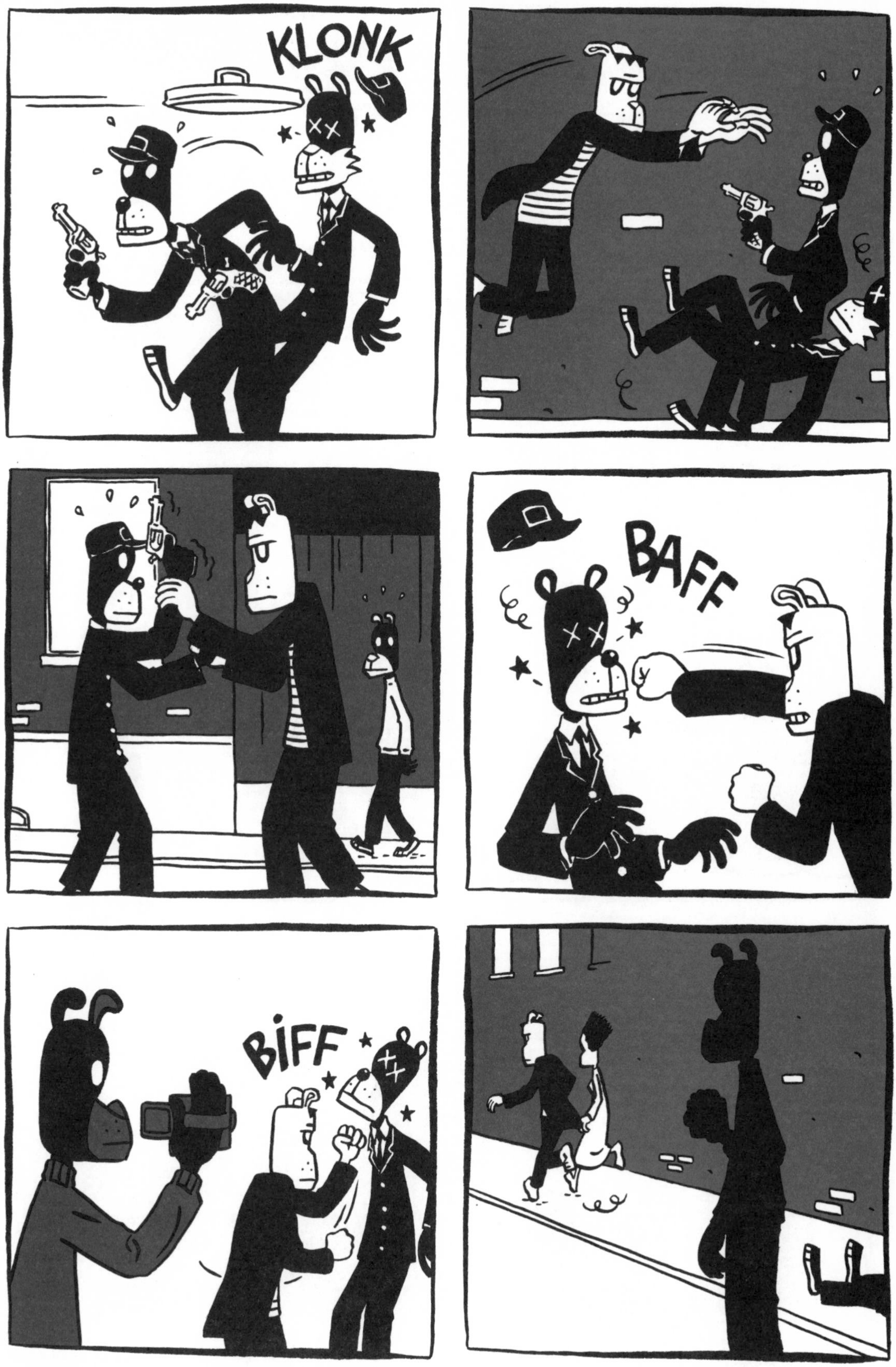
KLONK
BAFF
BIFF

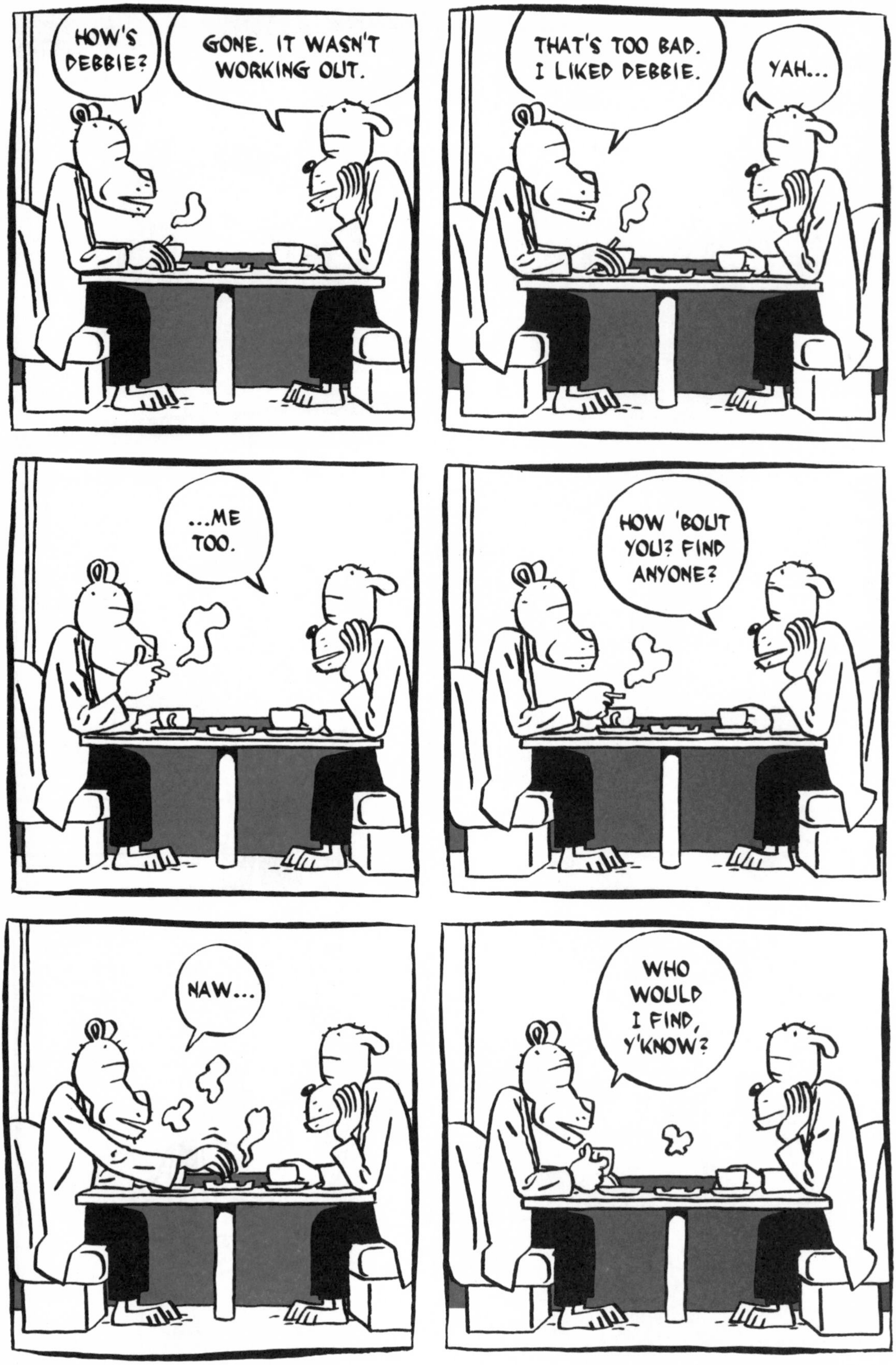
HOW'S DEBBIE?
GONE. IT WASN'T WORKING OUT.
THAT'S TOO BAD. I LIKED DEBBIE.
YAH...
...ME TOO.
HOW 'BOUT YOU? FIND ANYONE?
NAW...
WHO WOULD I FIND, Y'KNOW?

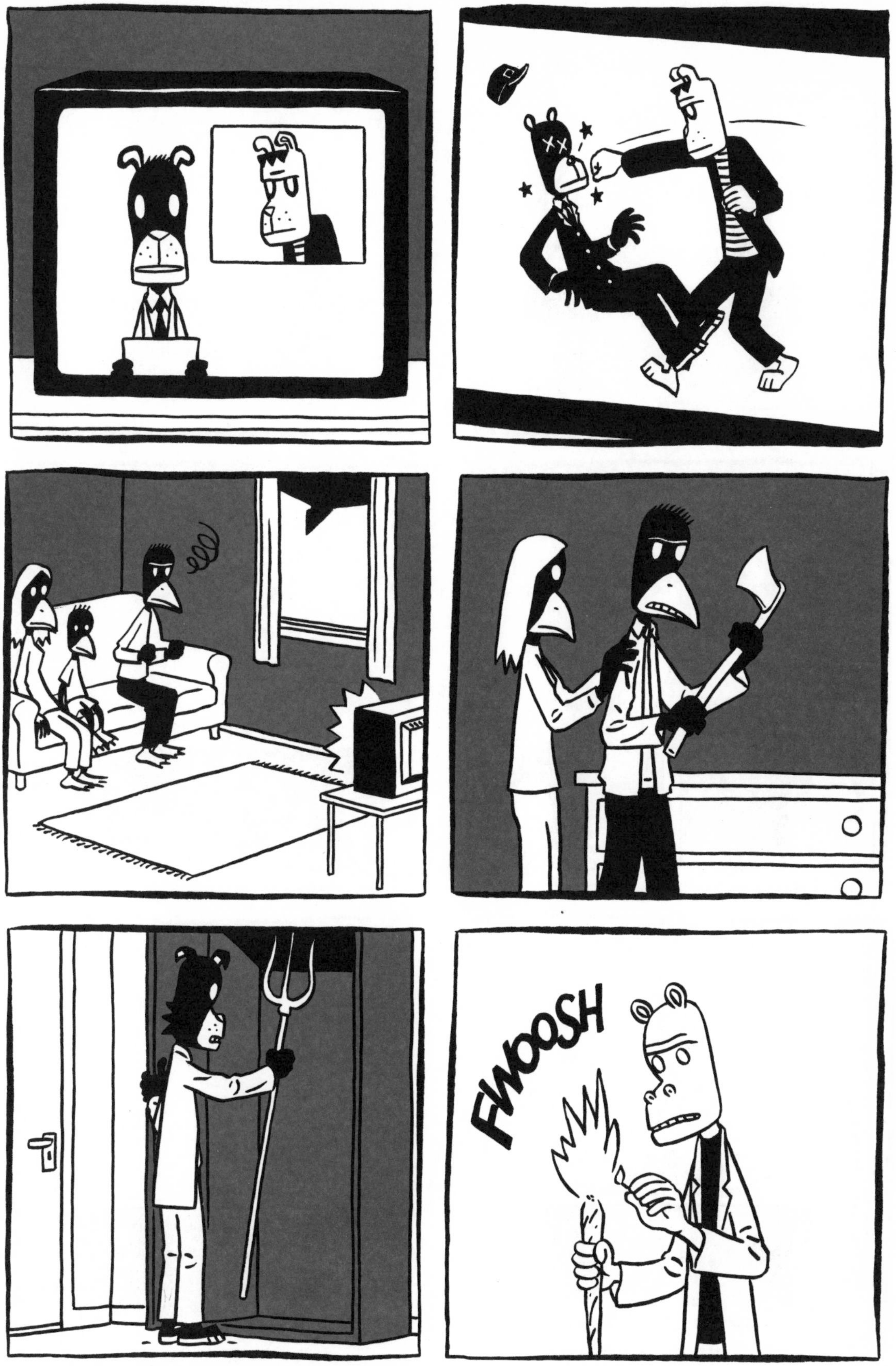
FWOOSH

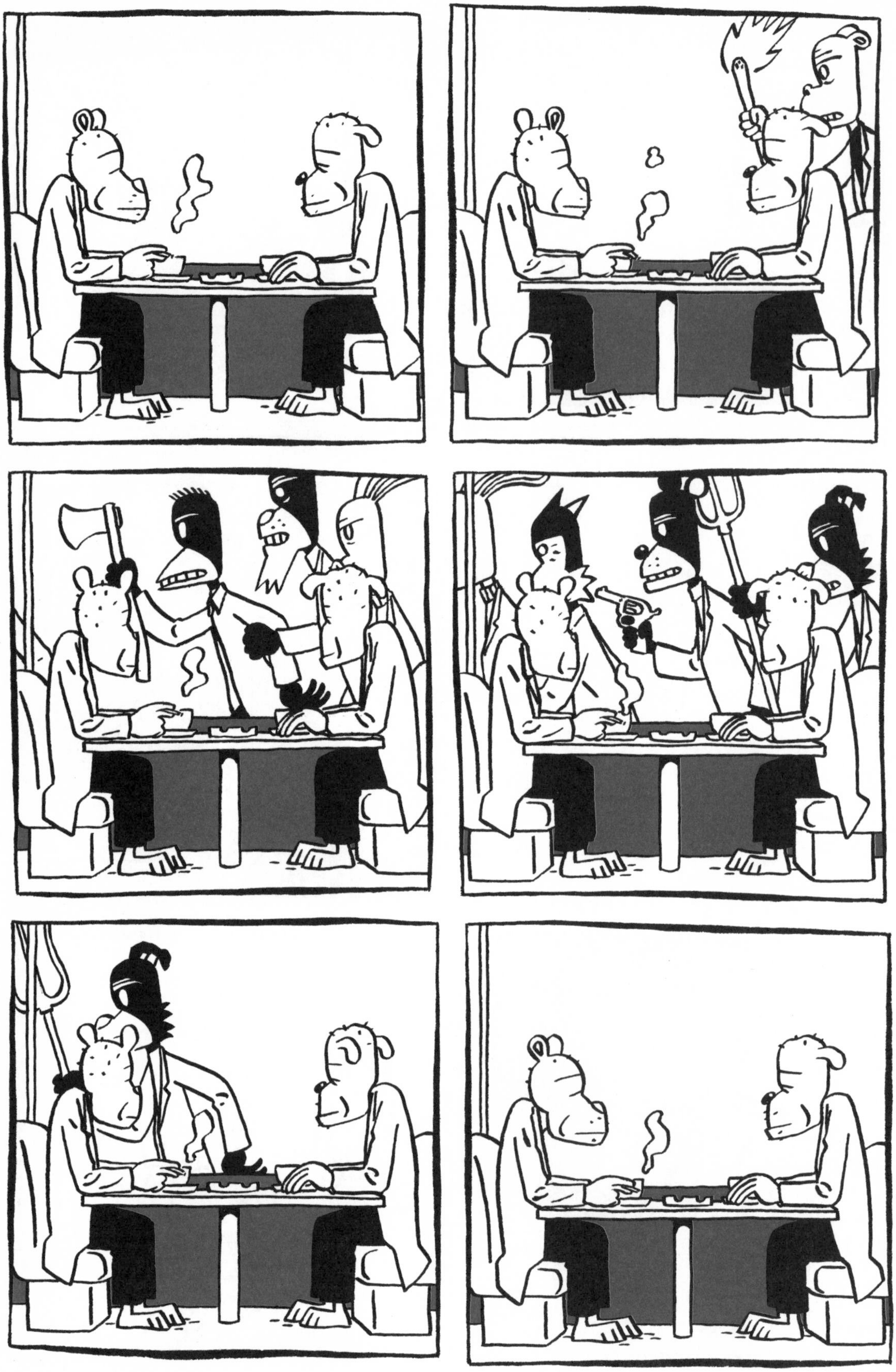

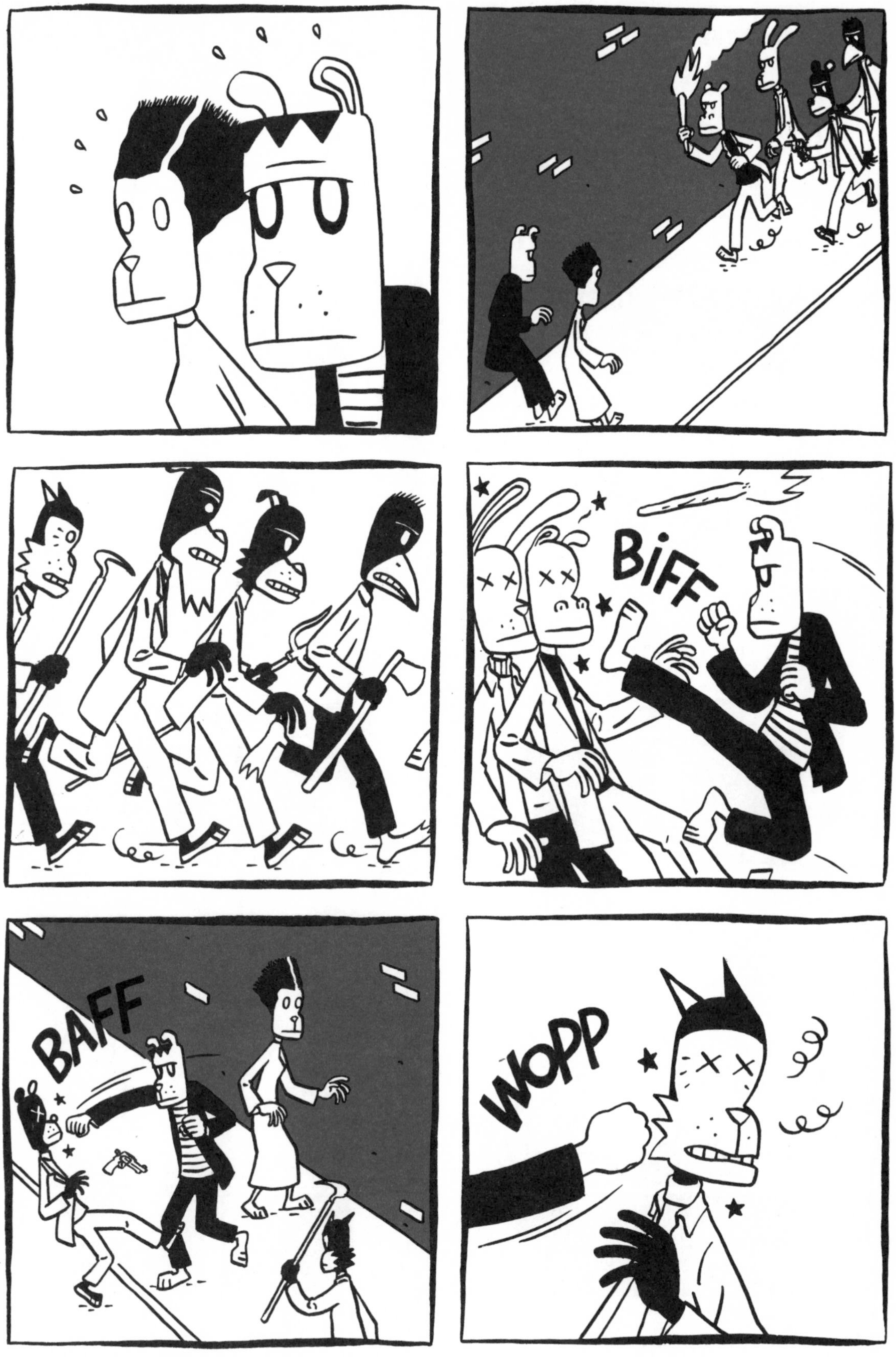
BiFF
BAFF
WOPP

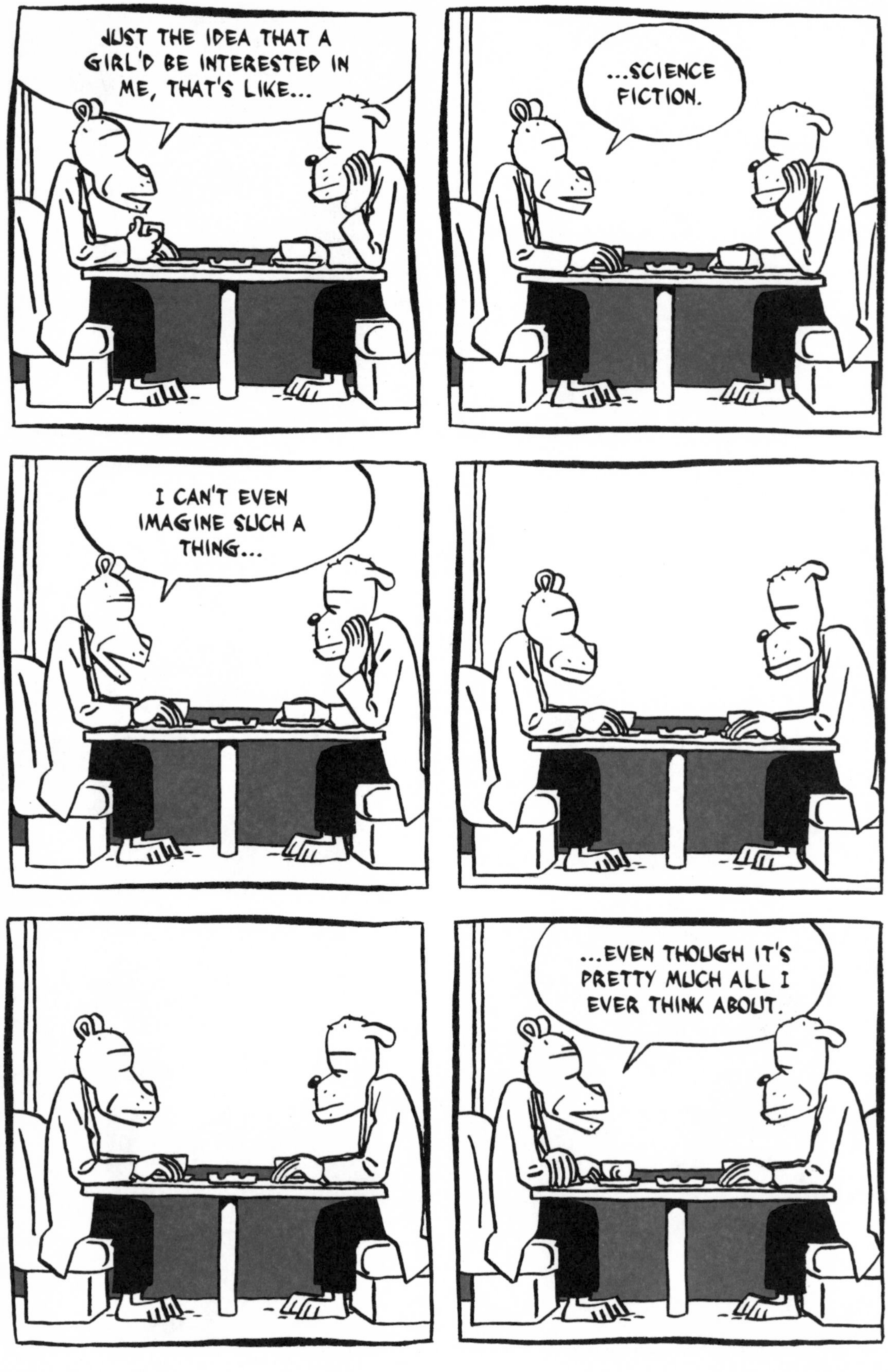
JUST THE IDEA THAT A GIRL'D BE INTERESTED IN ME, THAT'S LIKE...
...SCIENCE FICTION.
I CAN'T EVEN IMAGINE SUCH A THING...
...EVEN THOUGH IT'S PRETTY MUCH ALL I EVER THINK ABOUT.

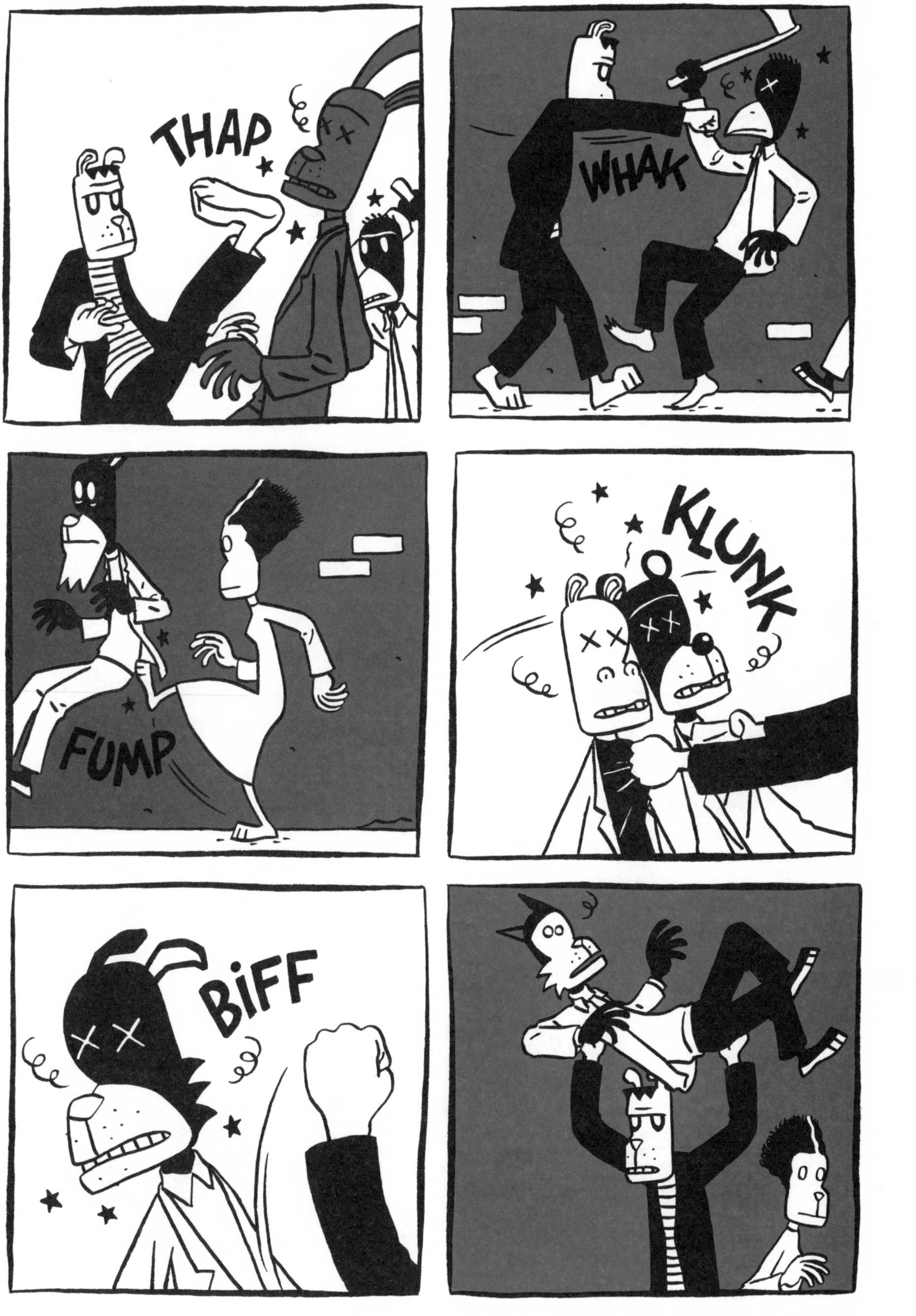
THAP
WHAK
FUMP
KLUNK
BIFF

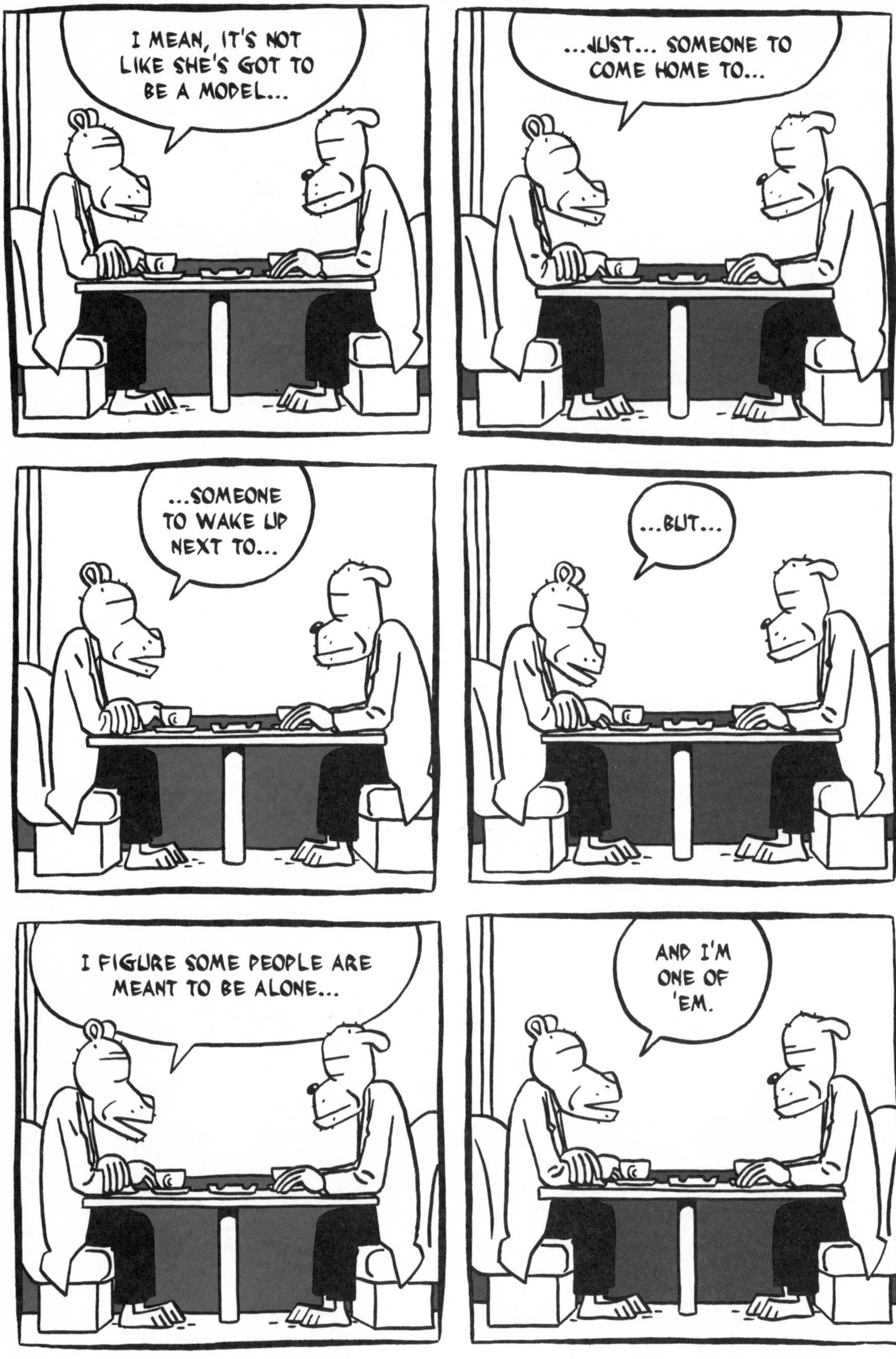
I MEAN, IT'S NOT LIKE SHE'S GOT TO BE A MODEL...
...JUST... SOMEONE TO COME HOME TO...
...SOMEONE TO WAKE UP NEXT TO...
...BUT...
I FIGURE SOME PEOPLE ARE MEANT TO BE ALONE...
AND I'M ONE OF 'EM.

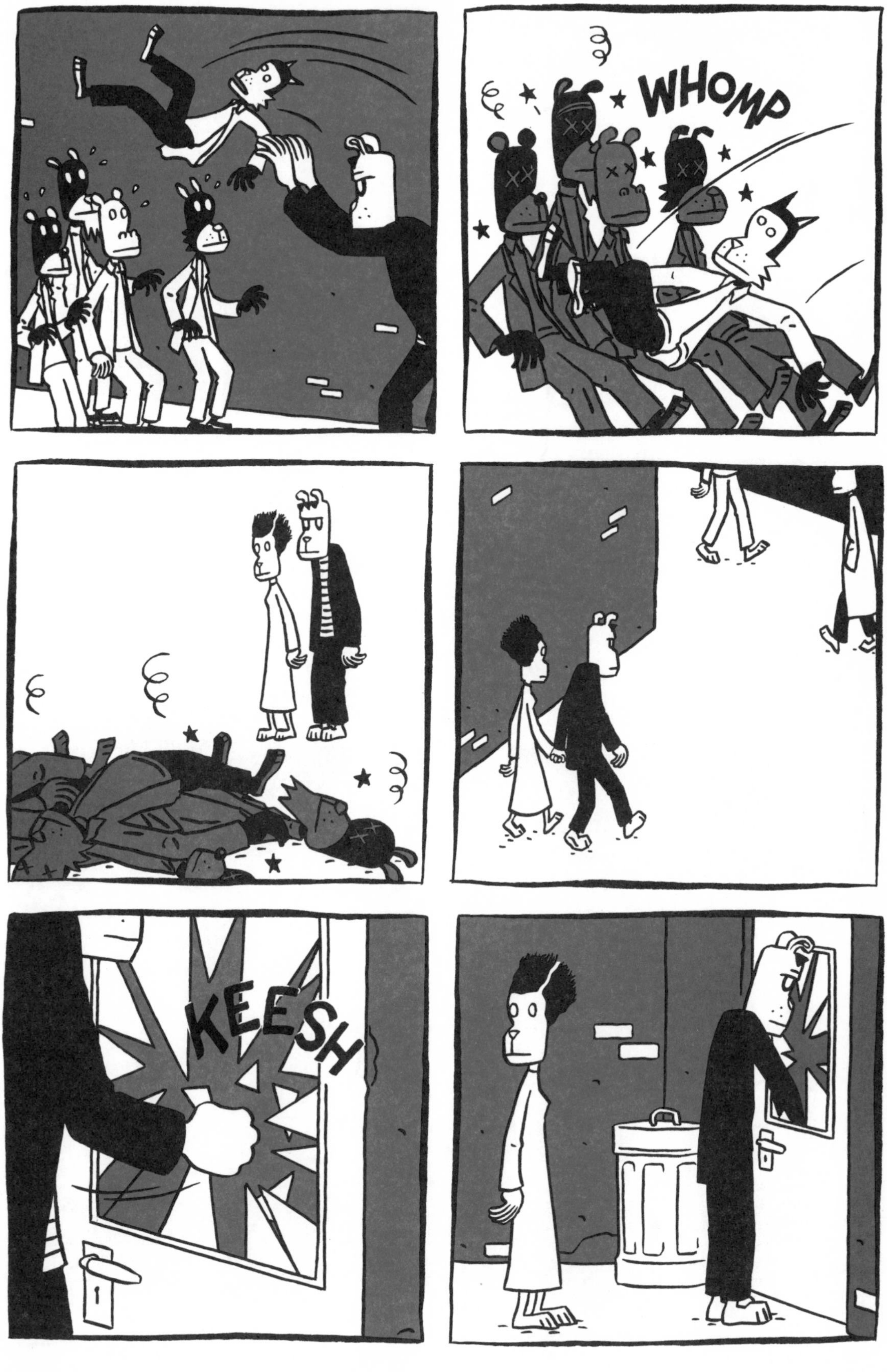
WHOMP
KEESH

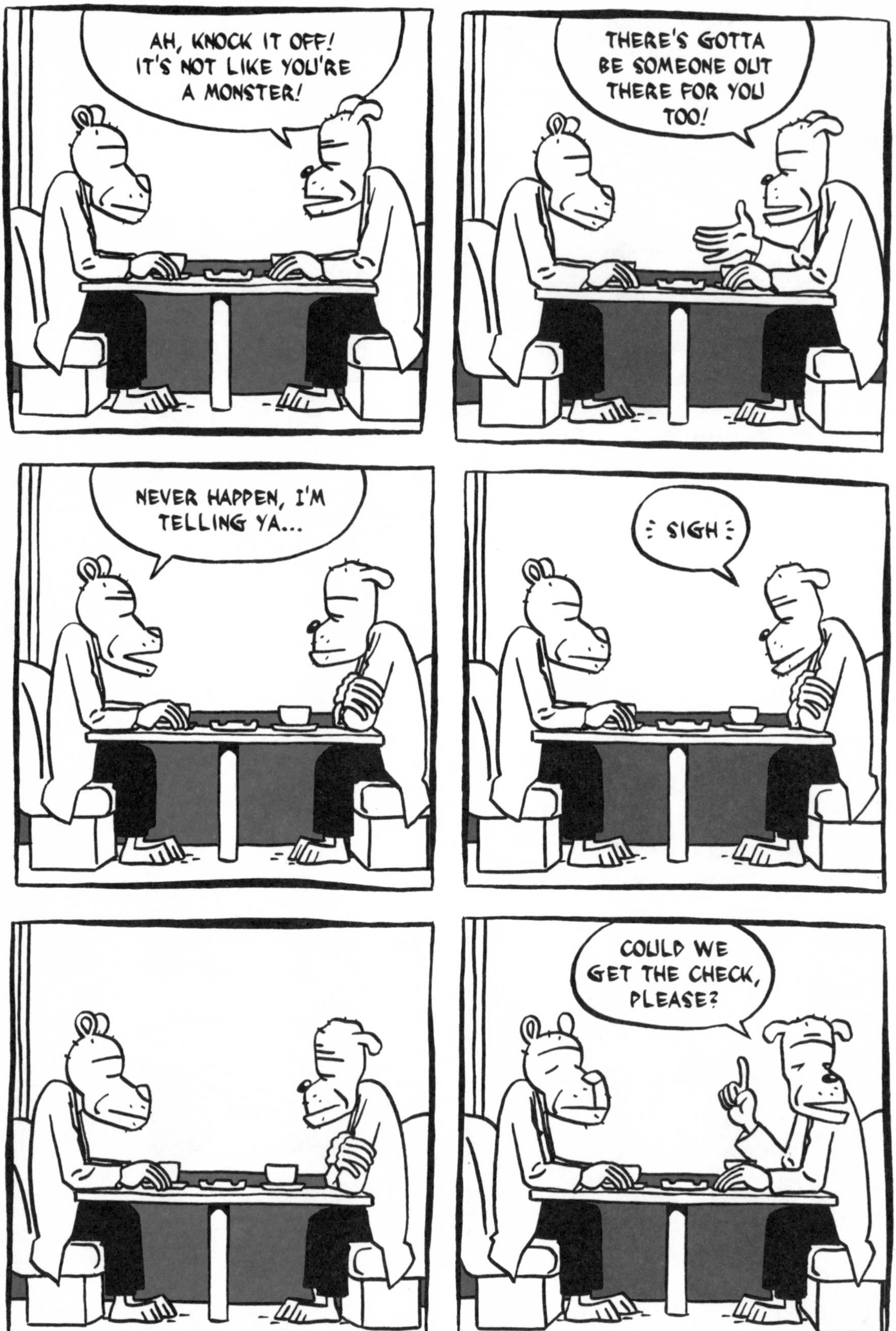
AH, KNOCK IT OFF! IT'S NOT LIKE YOU'RE A MONSTER!
THERE'S GOTTA BE SOMEONE OUT THERE FOR YOU TOO!
NEVER HAPPEN, I'M TELLING YA...
SIGH
COULD WE GET THE CHECK, PLEASE?

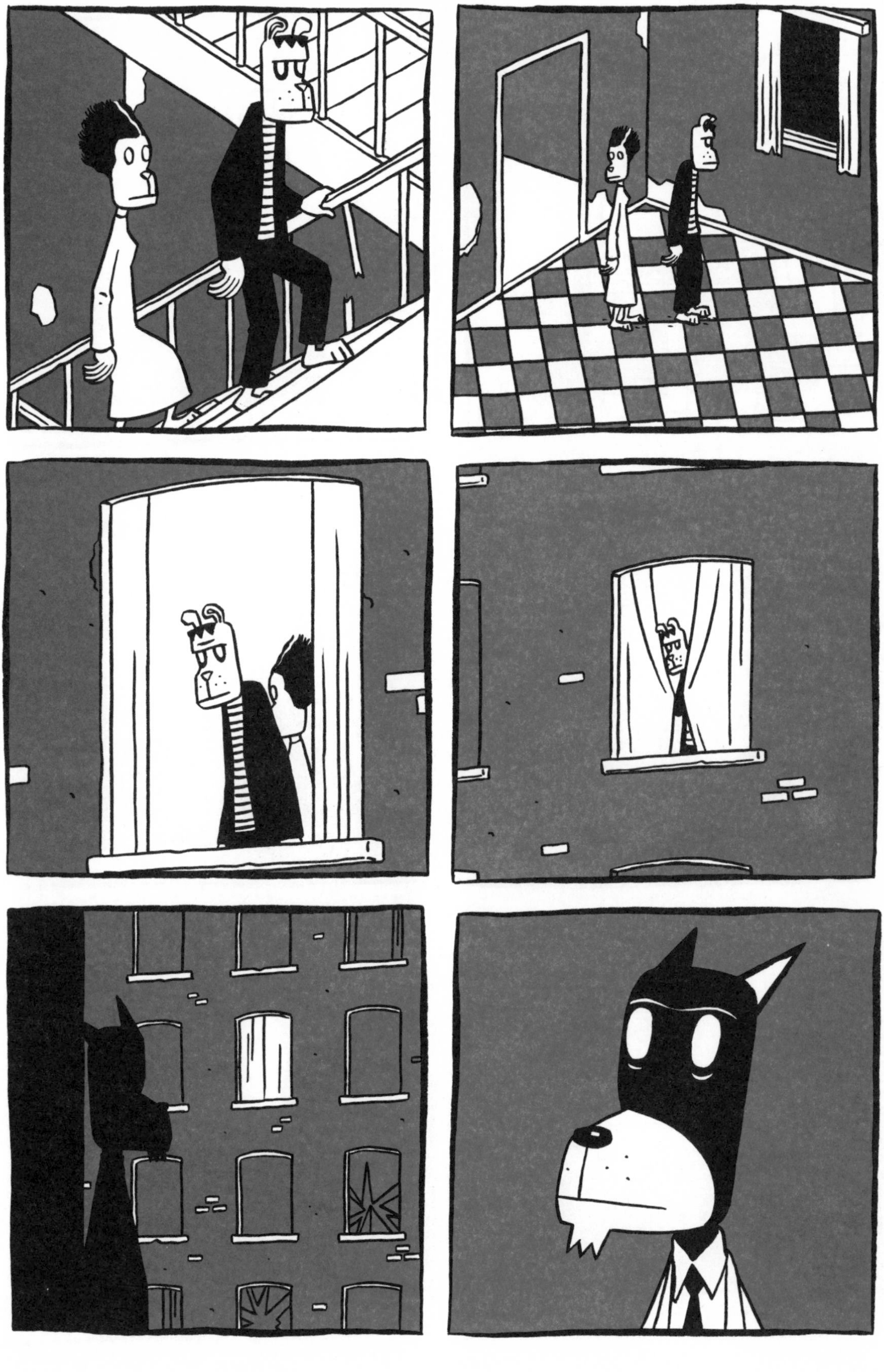

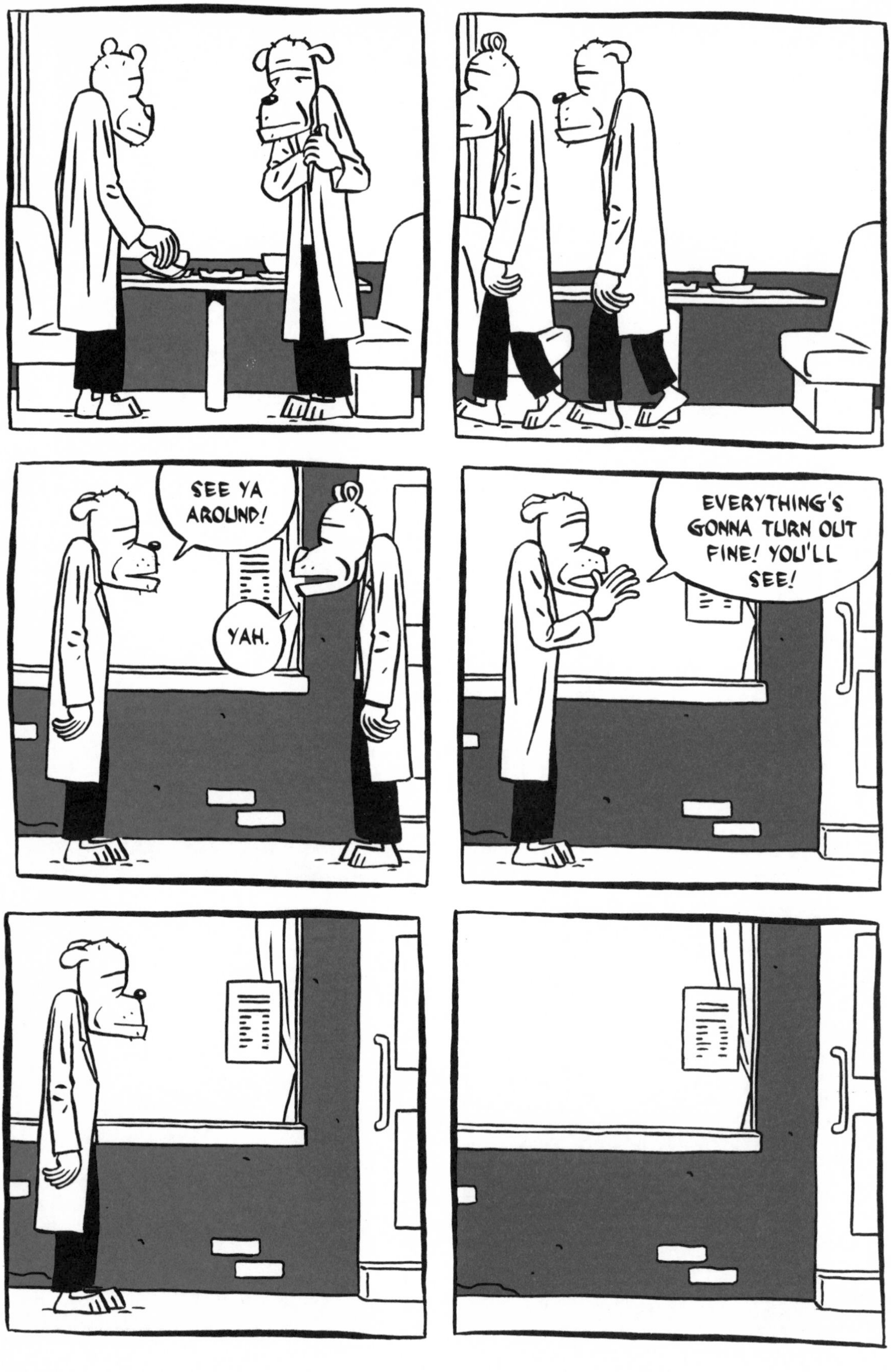
SEE YA AROUND!
YAH.
EVERYTHING'S GONNA TURN OUT FINE! YOU'LL SEE!

THREE

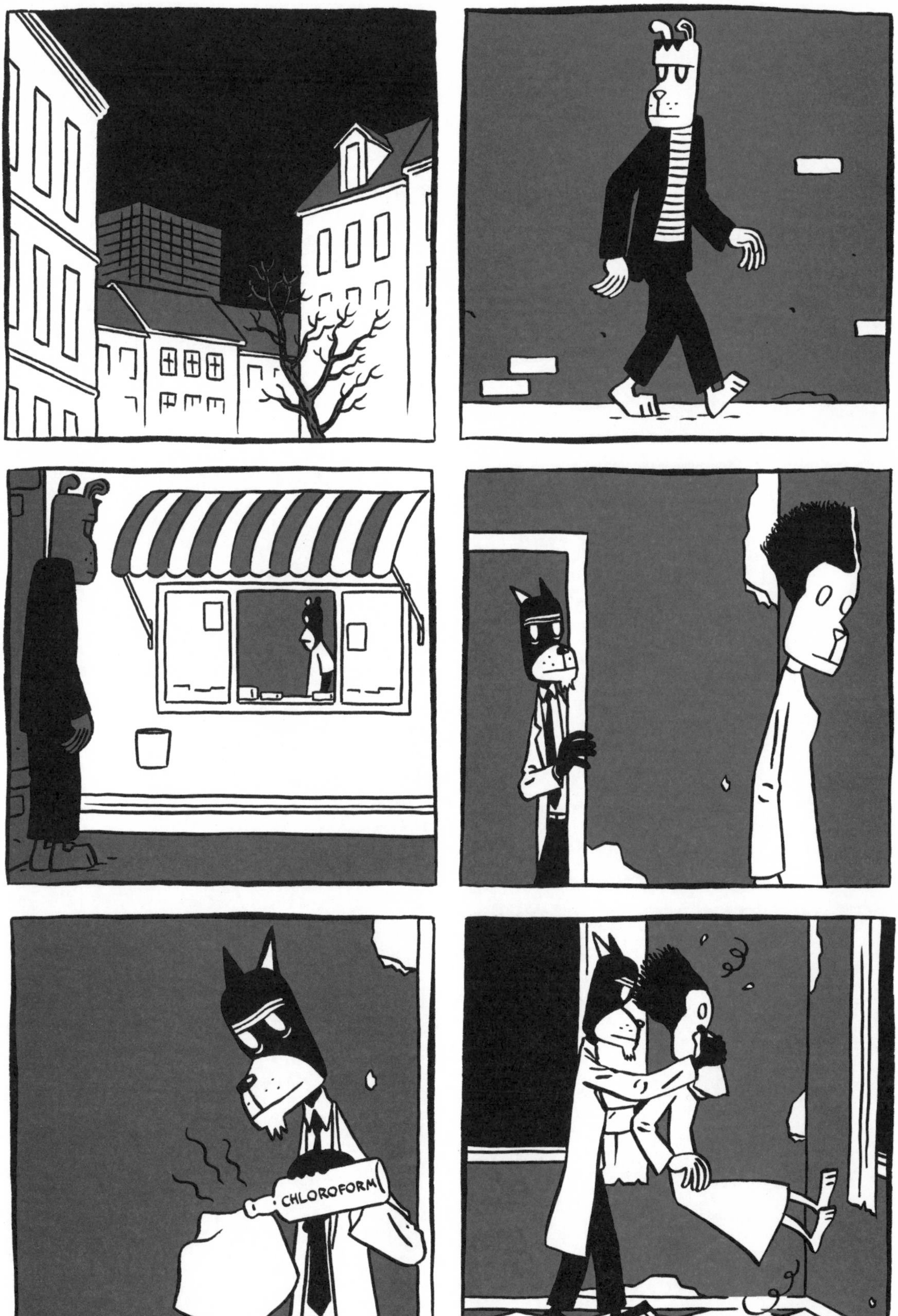
CHLOROFORM

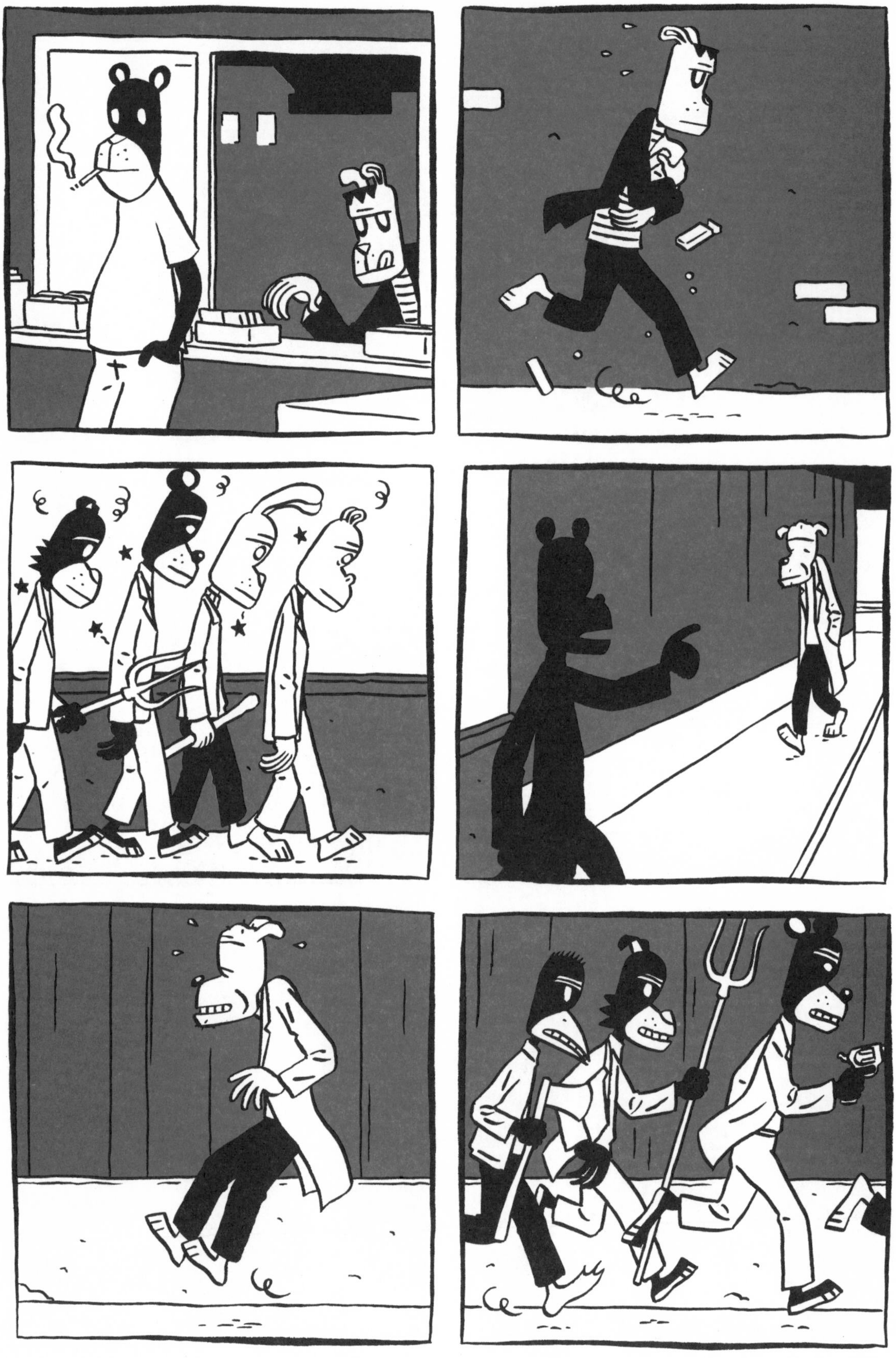

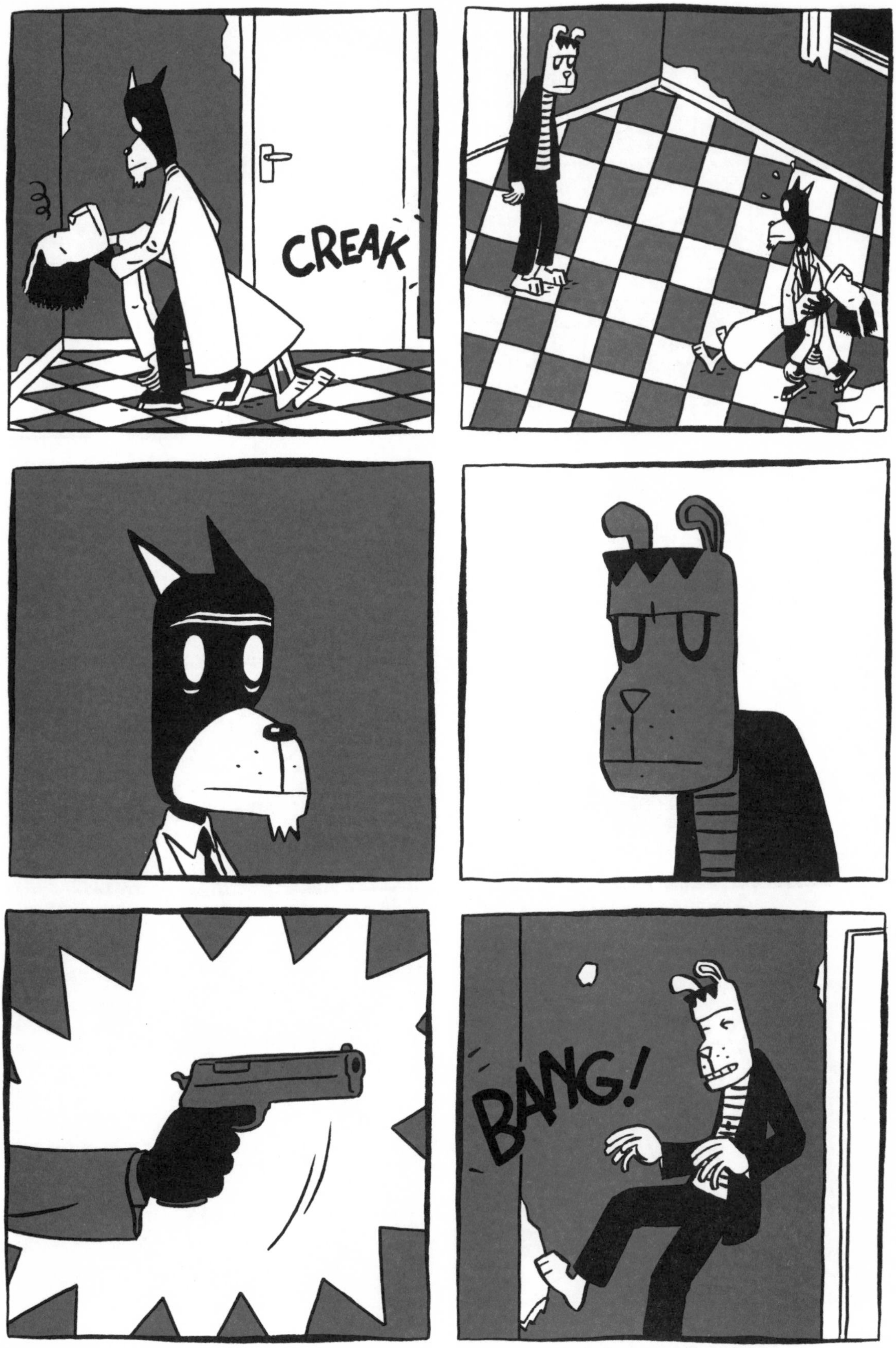
CREAK
BANG!

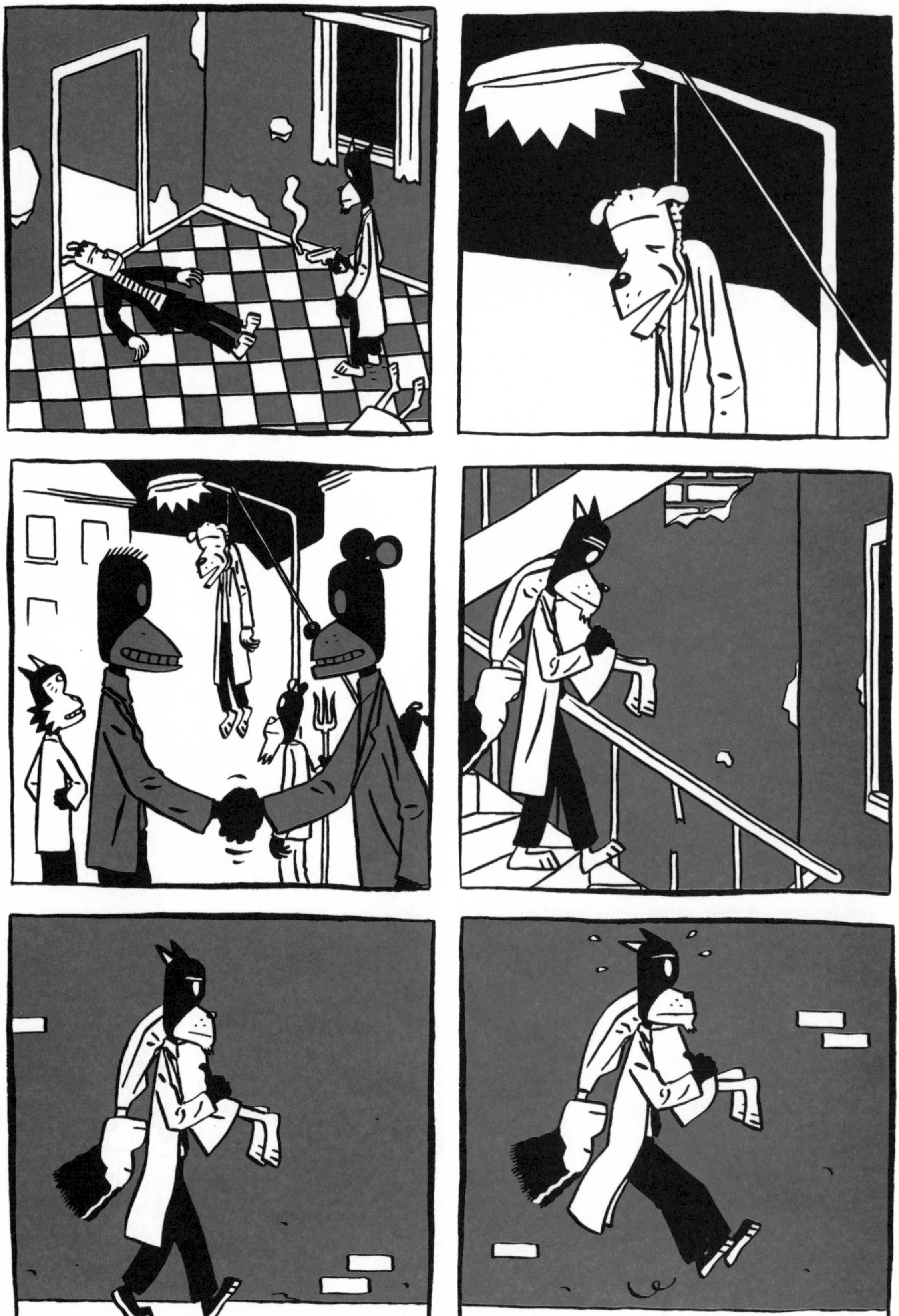

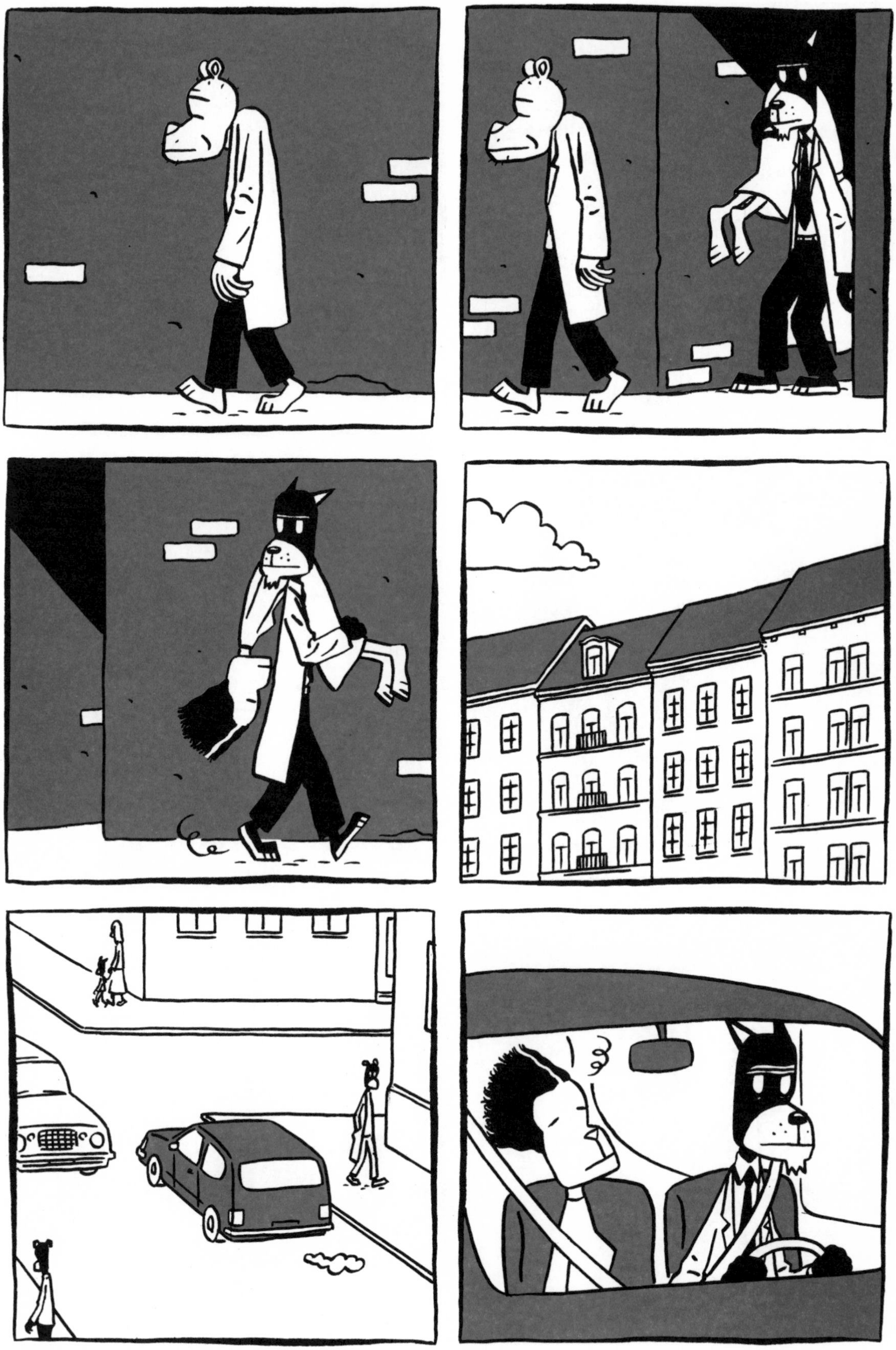

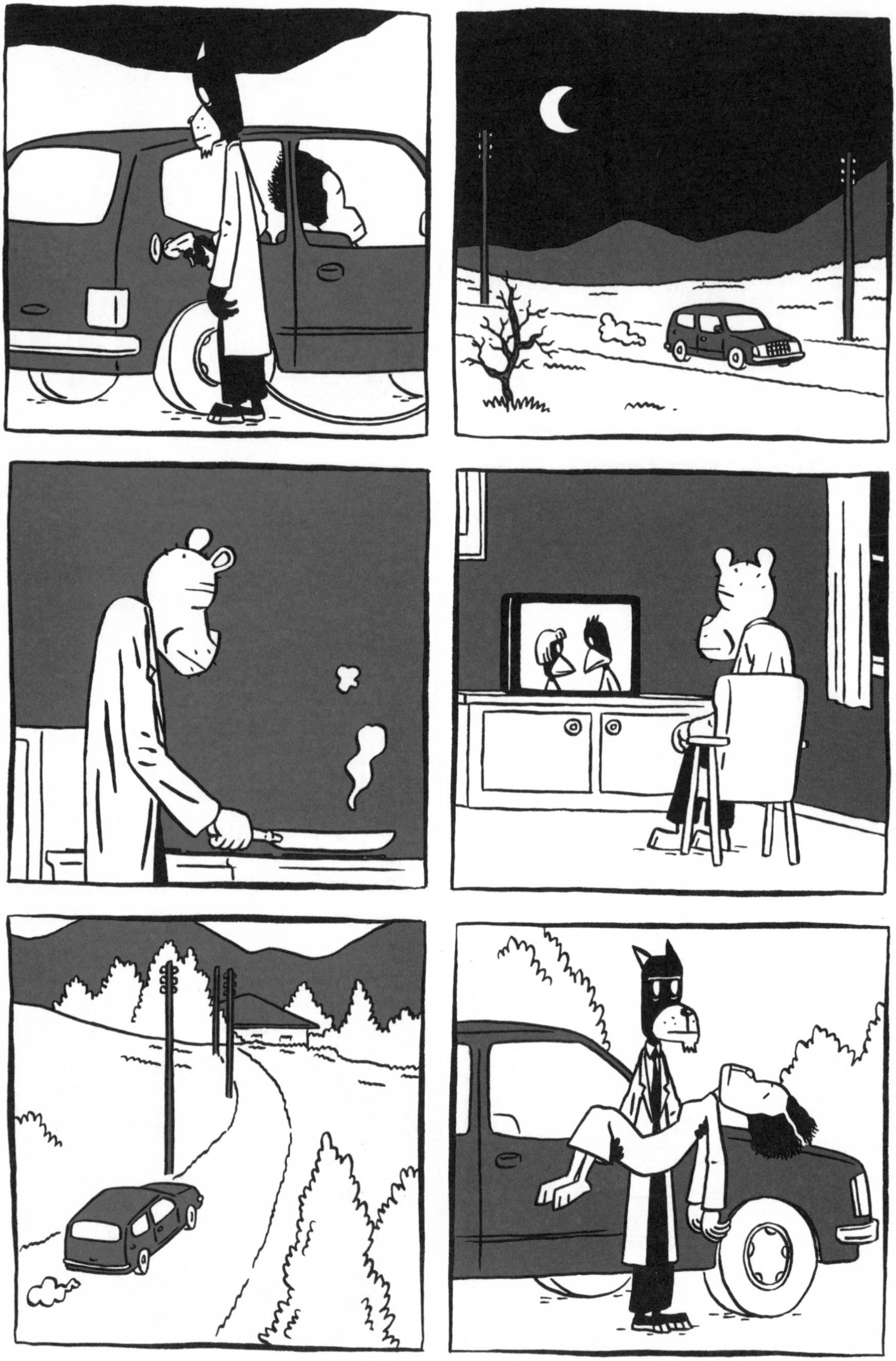

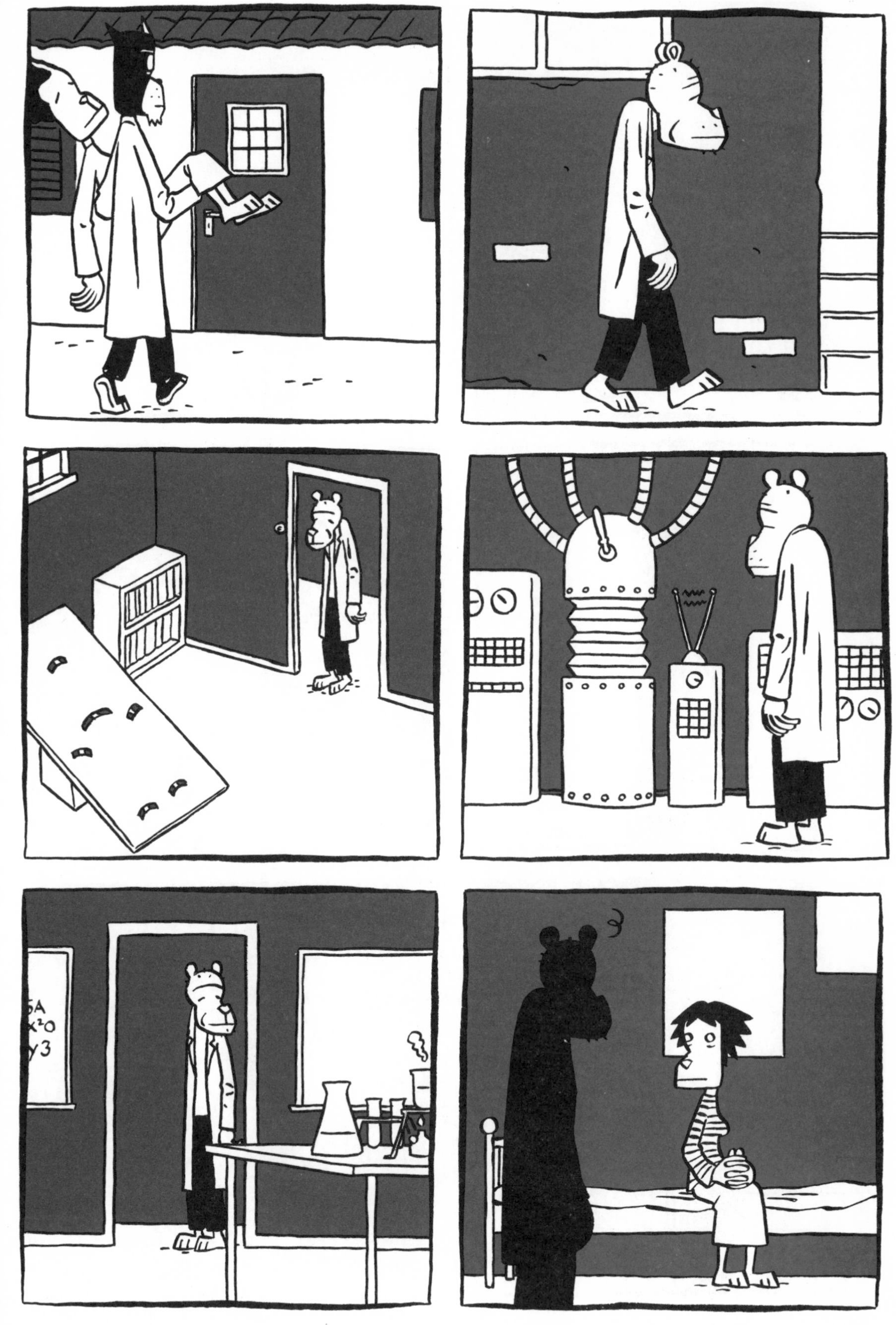

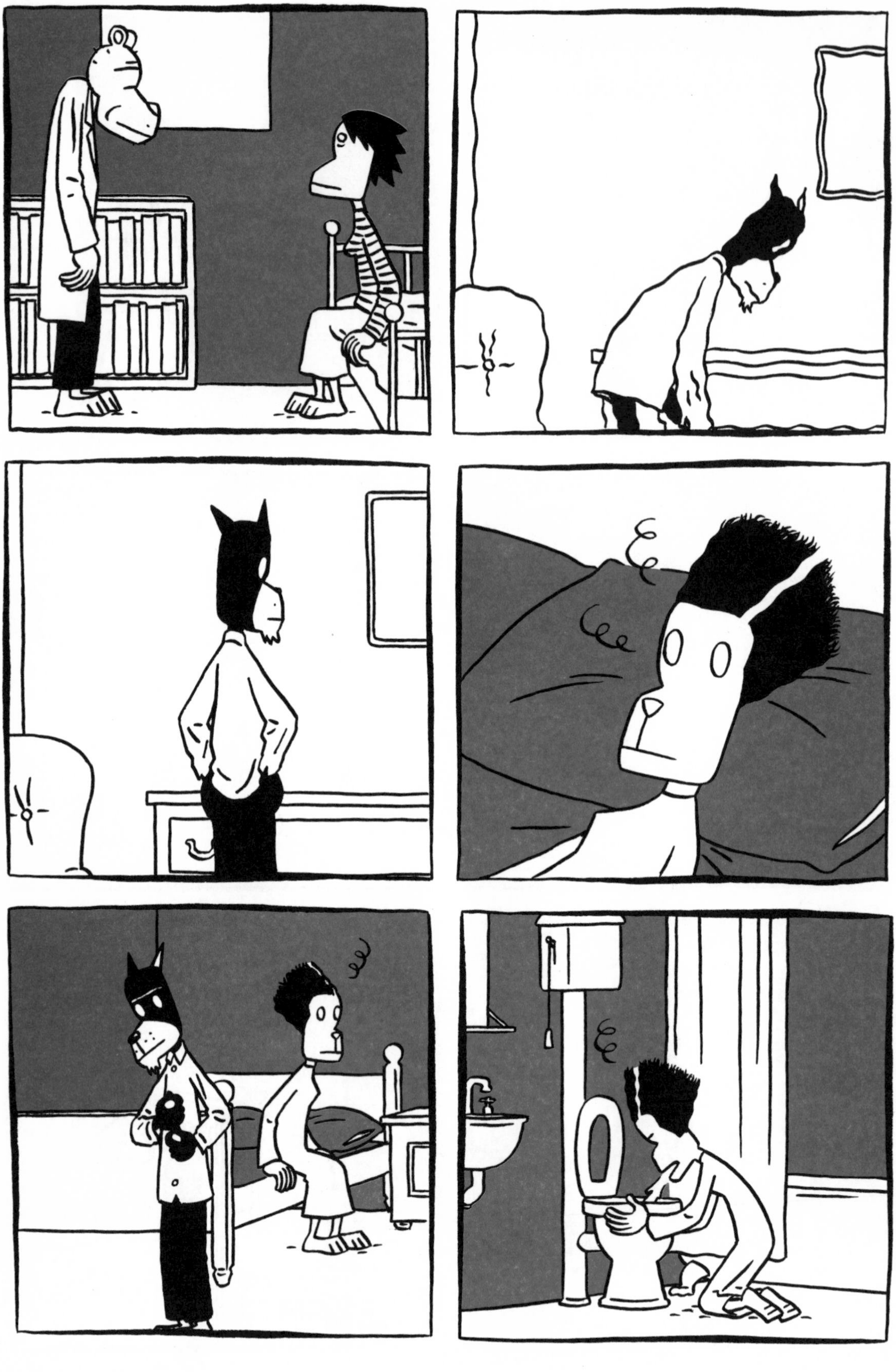

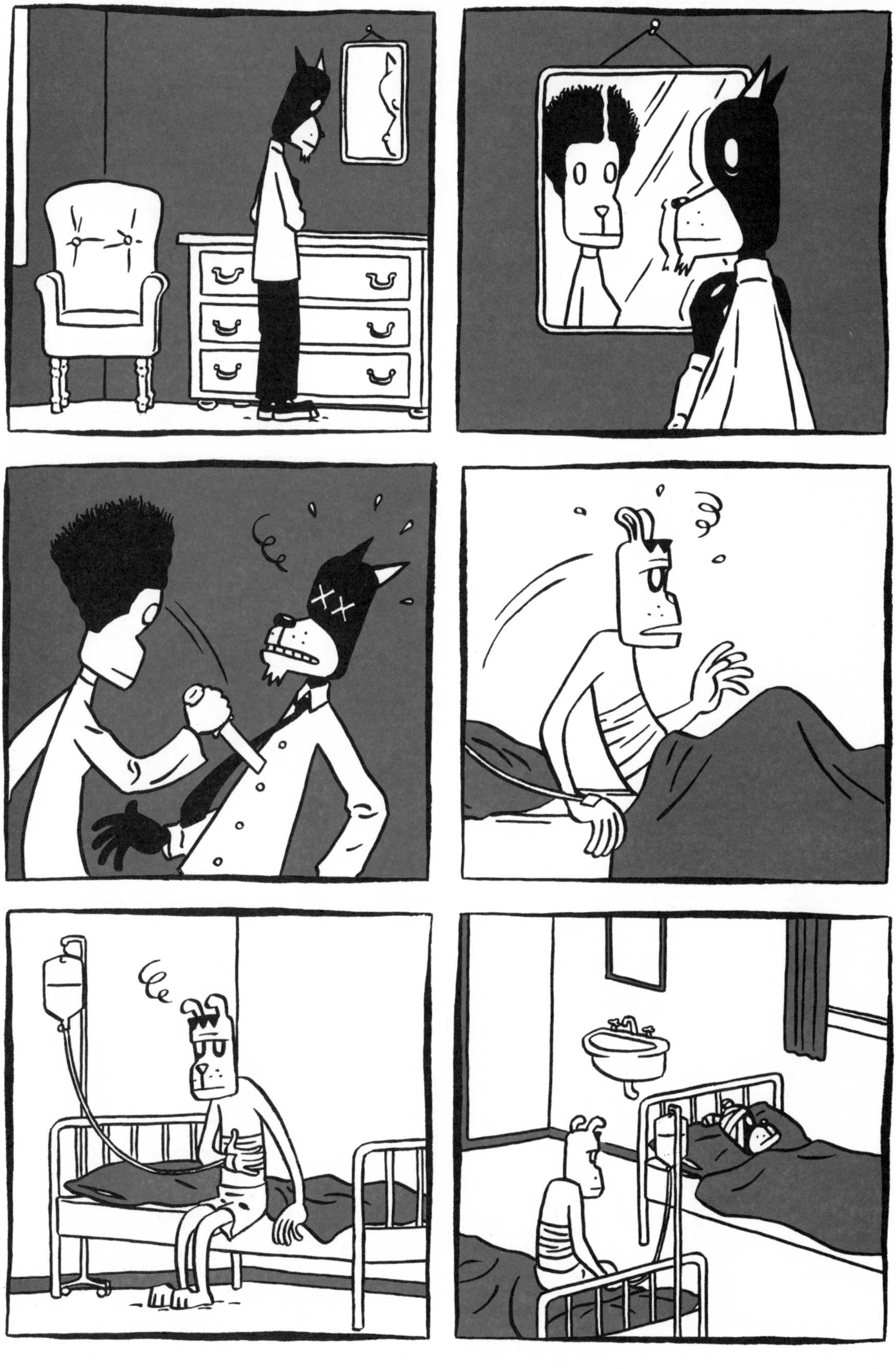

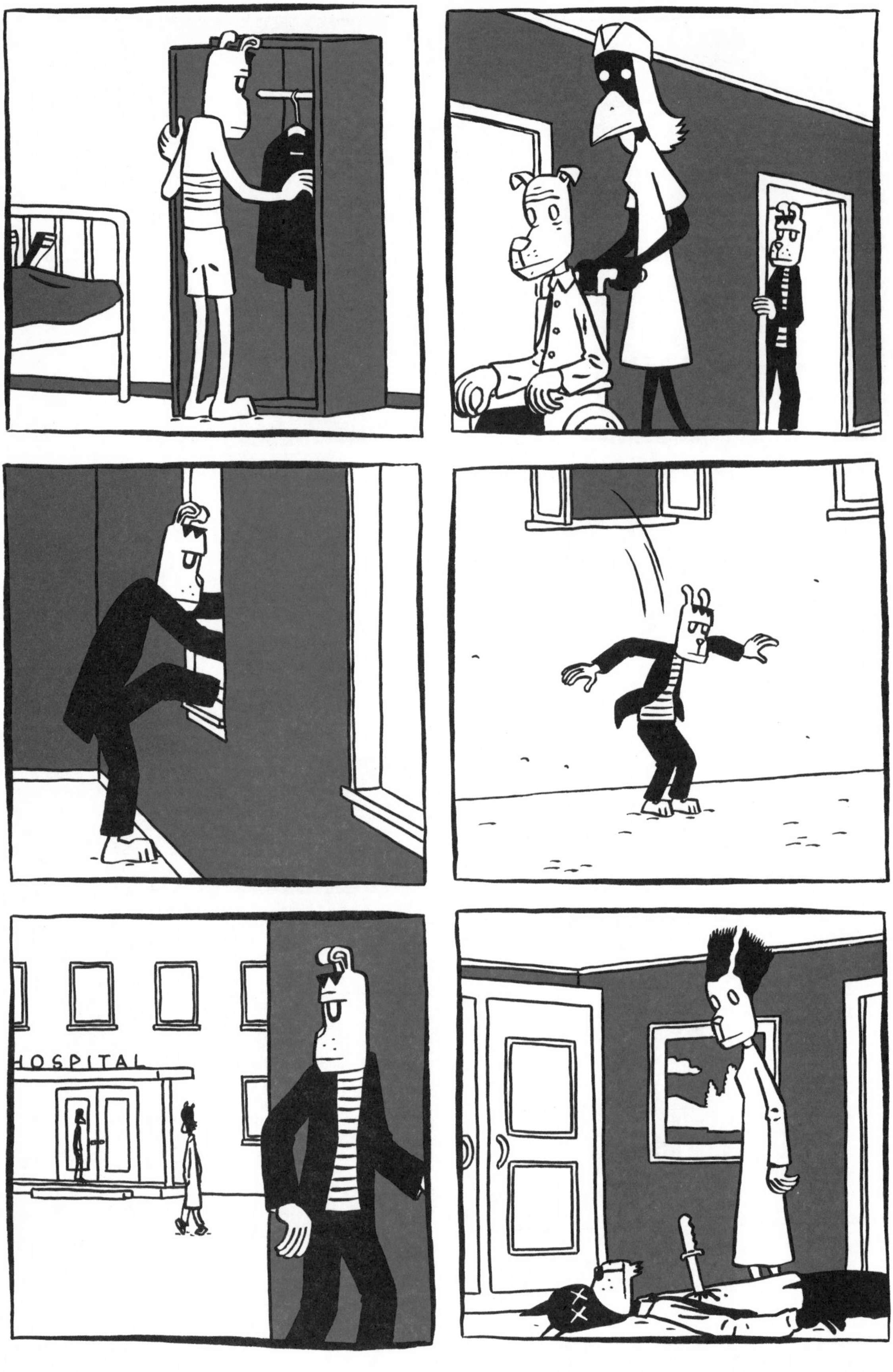
HOSPITAL

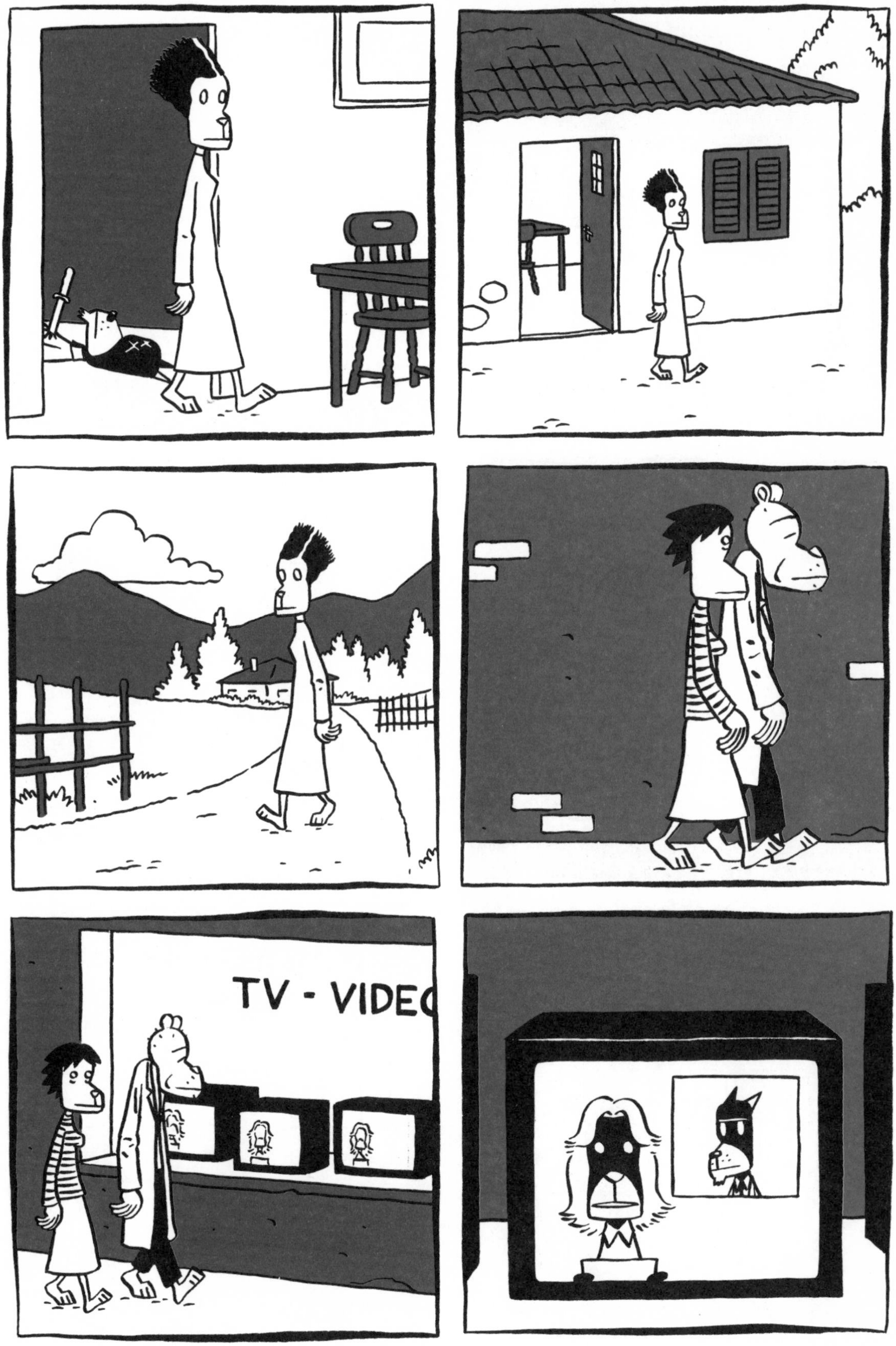
TV - VIDE

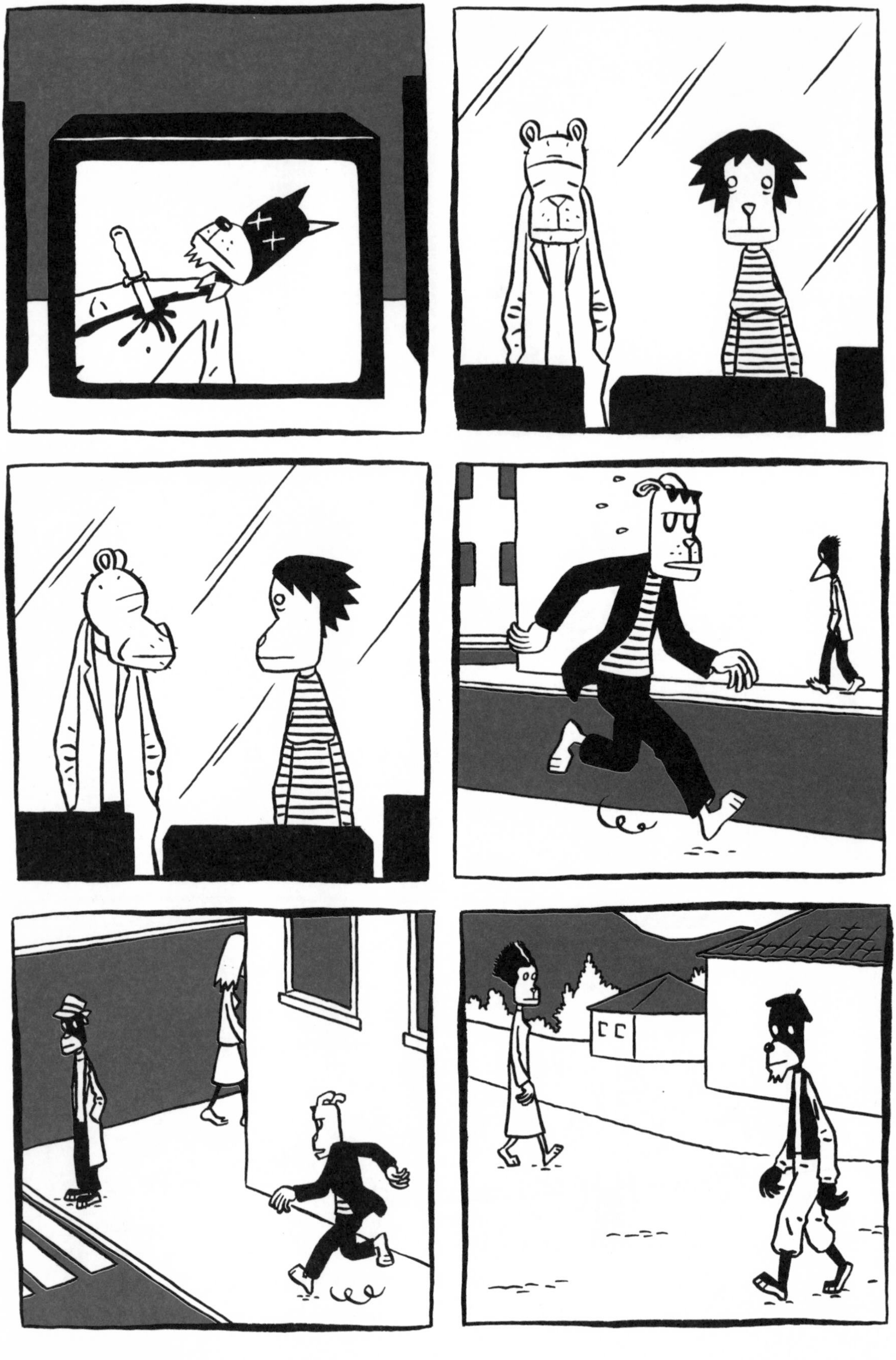

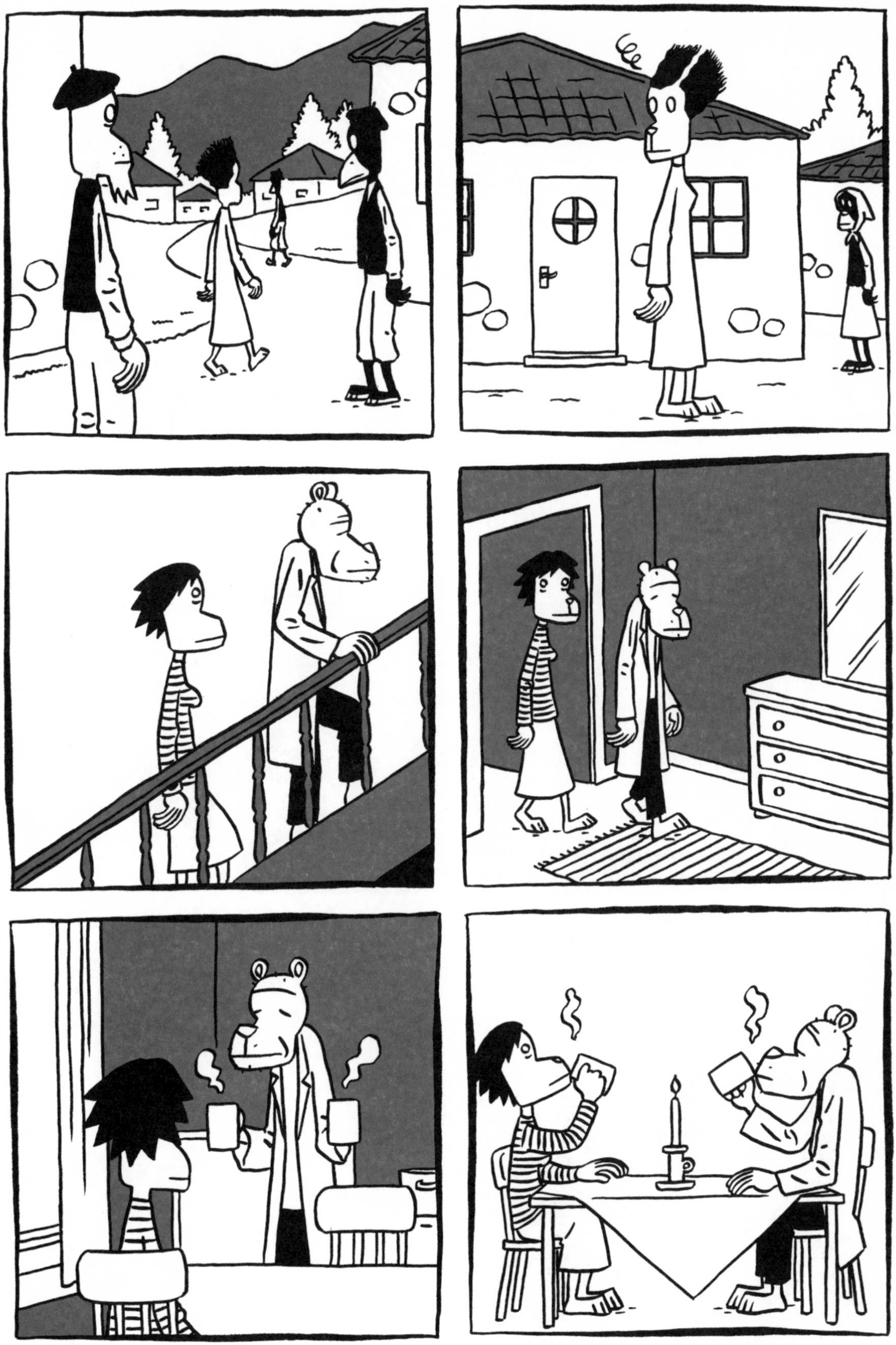

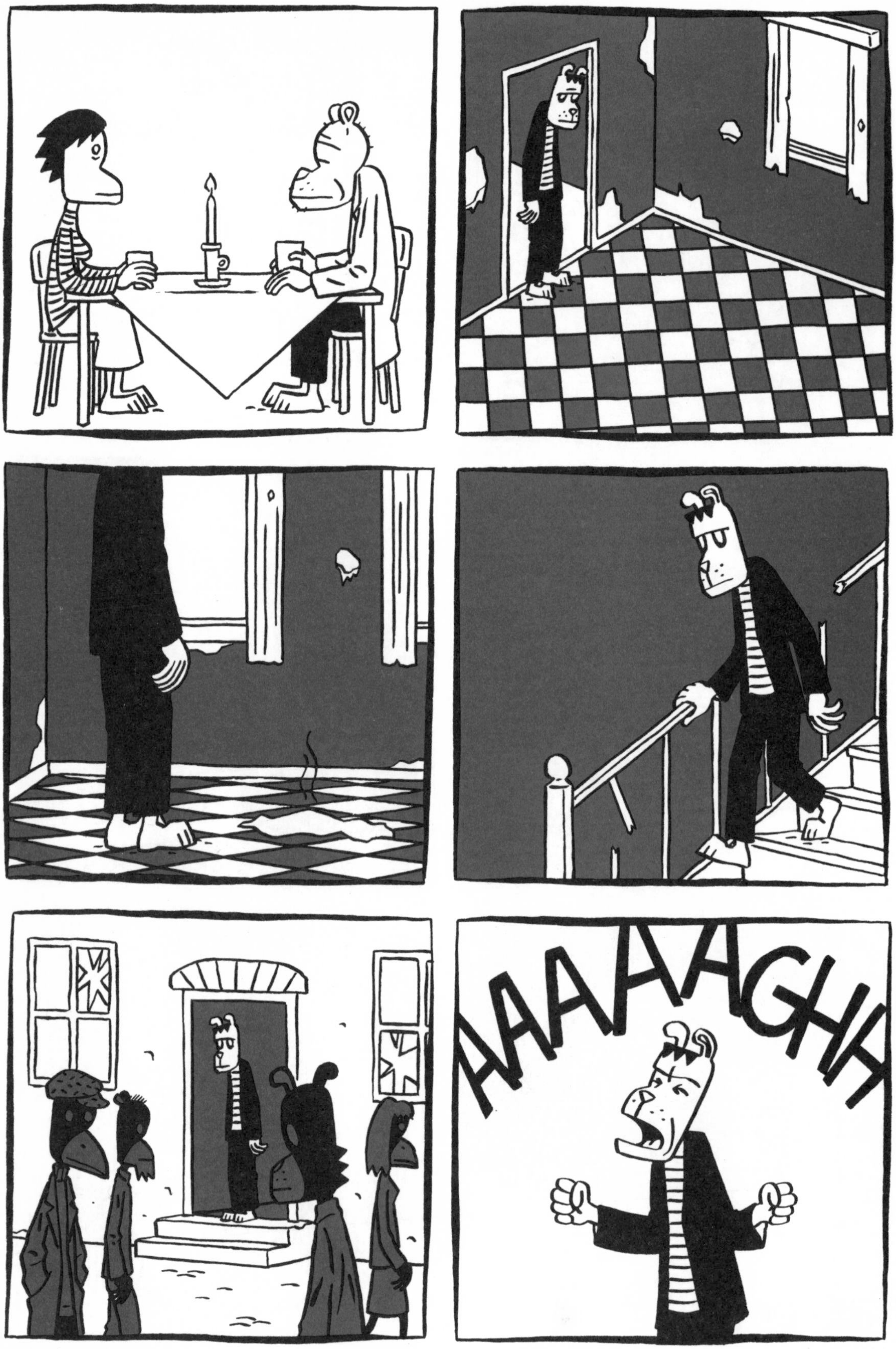
AAAAAGHH

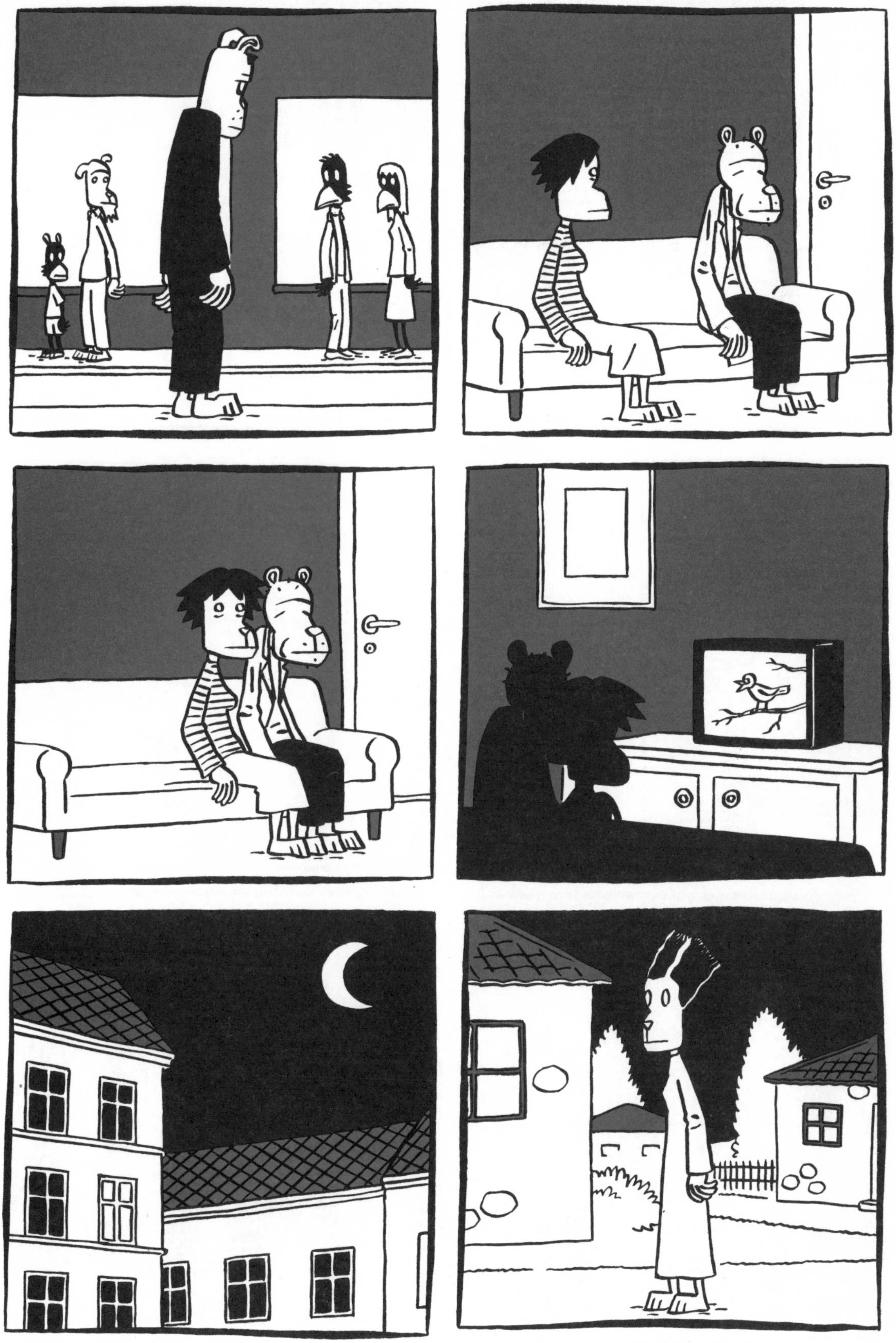

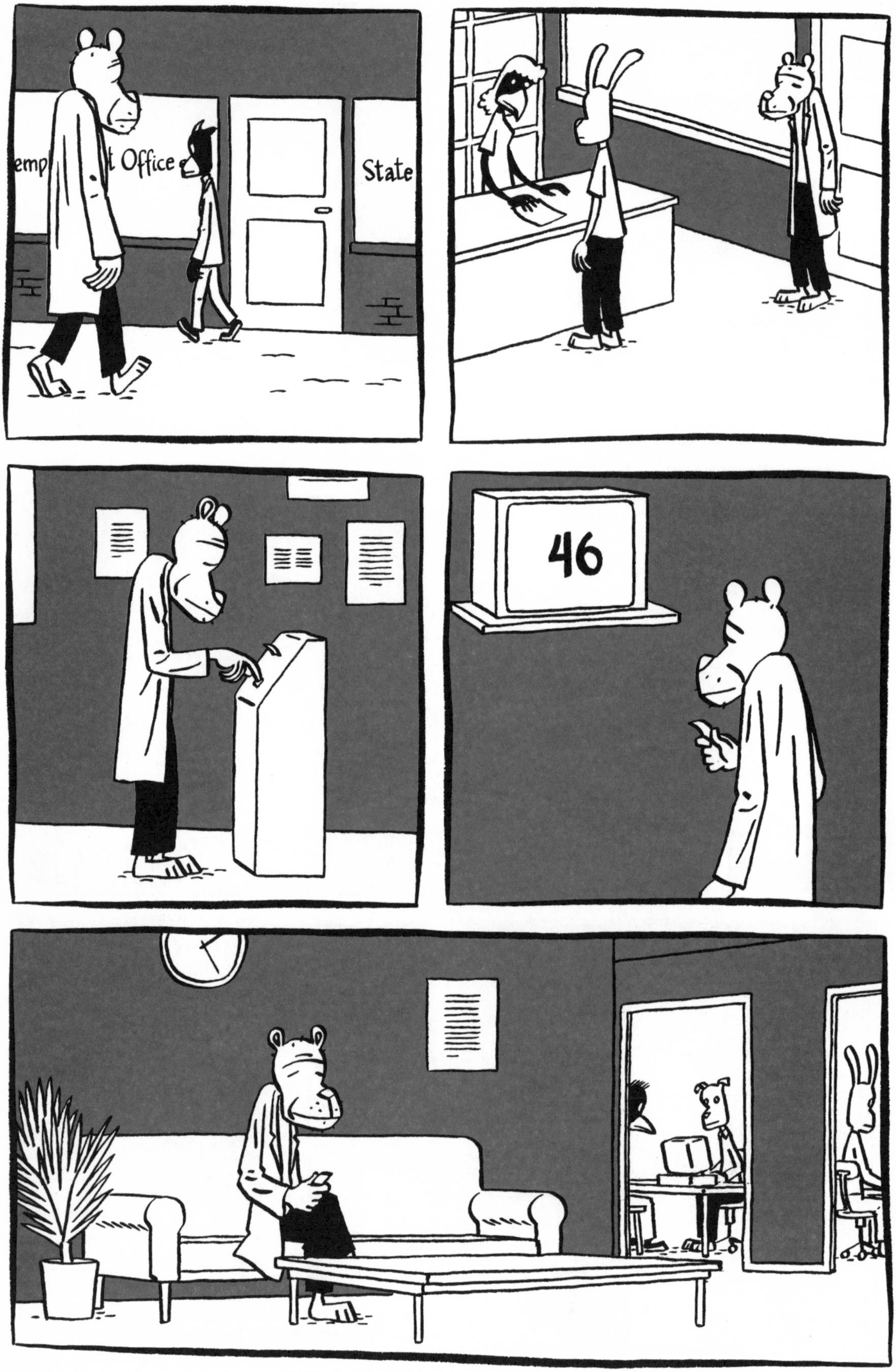
emp
t Office
State
46

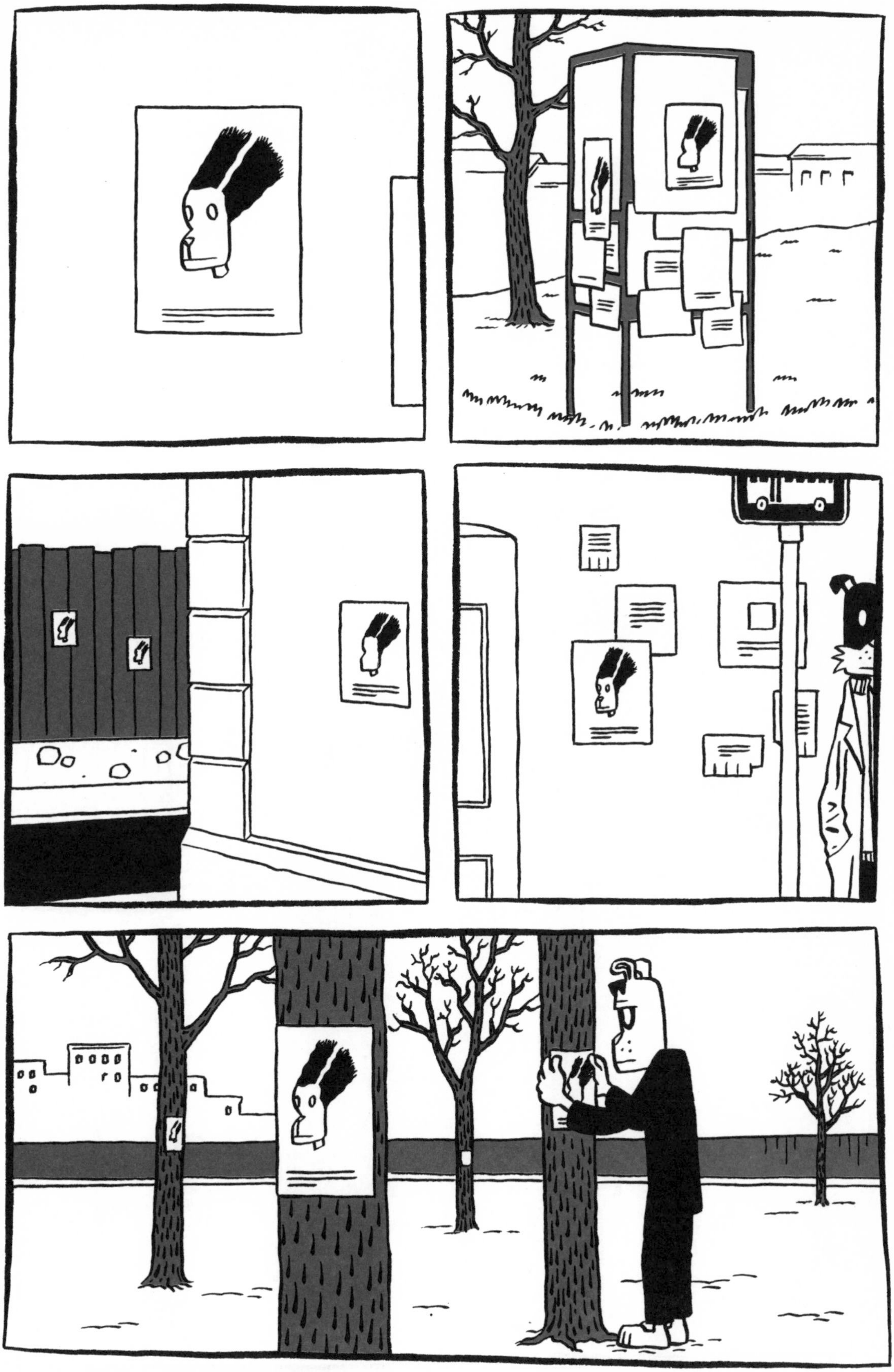

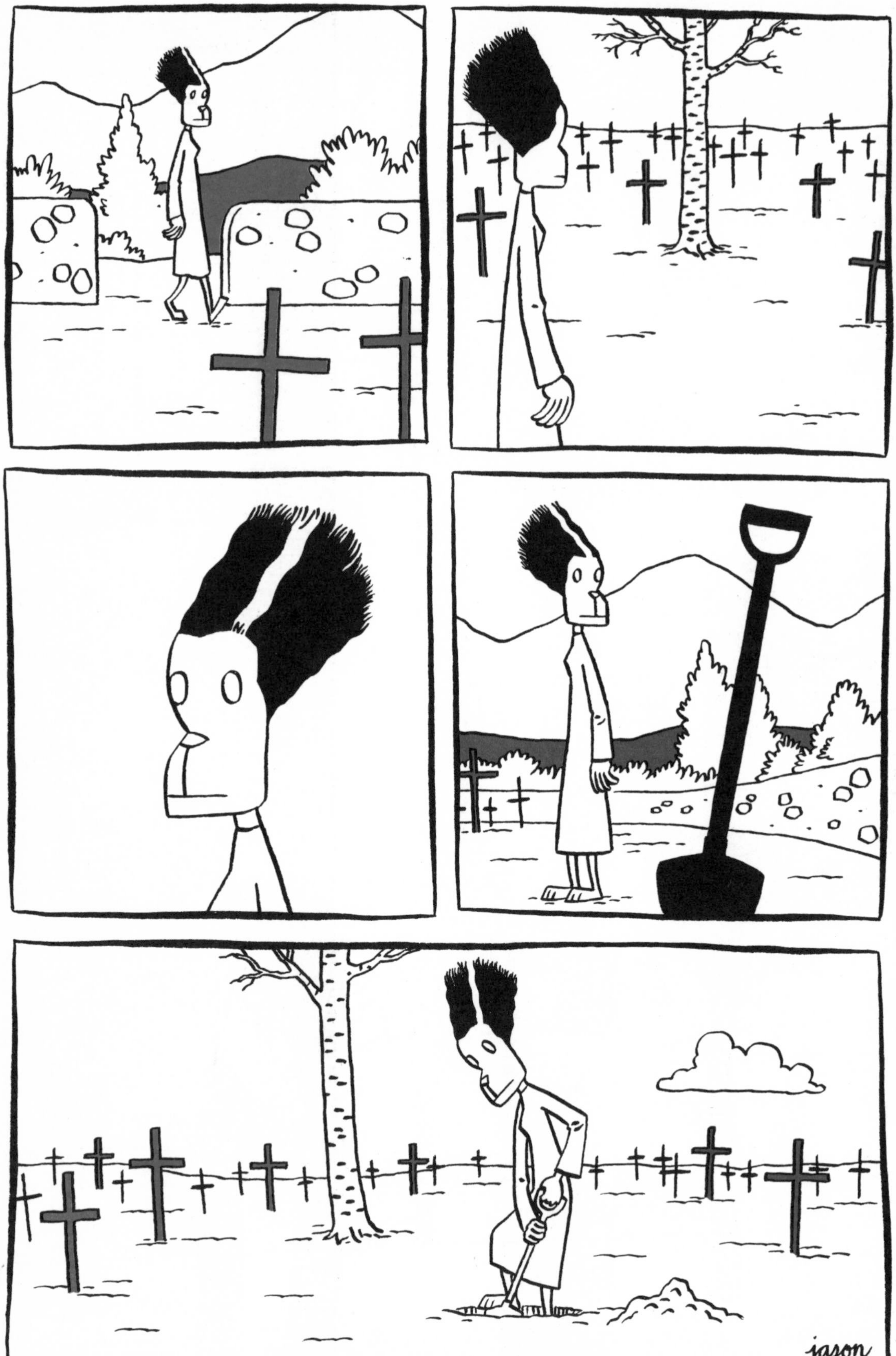
jason